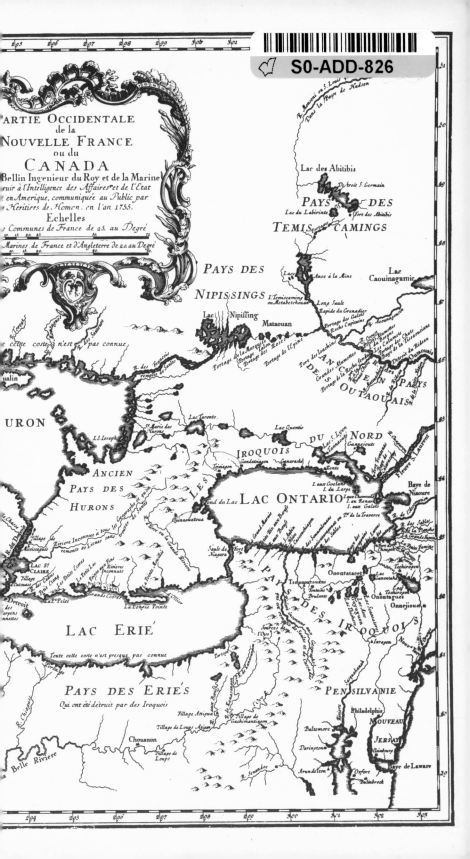

PARTIE OCCIDENTALE
de la
NOUVELLE FRANCE
ou du
CANADA
Bellin Ingenieur du Roy et de la Marine
_ruir à l'Intelligence des Affaires et de l'Etat
_ en Amerique, communiquée au Public par
_ Heritiers de Homen, en l'an 1755.
Echelles
_ Communes de France de 25. au Degré

_ Marines de France et d'Angleterre de 20. au Degré

Lac des Abitibis

Détroit S. Germain

PAYS DES
TEMIS CAMINGS

Lac du Labirinte     Fort des Abitibis

Lac Caouinagamic

PAYS DES
NIPISSINGS

Ance à la Mine

L: Temiscaming
ou Metabetchouan

Lac Nipissing

Matouan

Long Sault
Rapide du Grenadier
Portage des Galets
Roche Capitaine

Fort de Joachim
Grandes Hummetes
Portage de la Roche fendue
Portage Salon de Rost.

Portage de l'Epine

_ cette coste n'est pas connue

R. des François
remplit de Saults

ANCIEN PAYS
DES
OUTAOUAIS

Lac Taronto

Lac Quentio

DU NORD

HURON

St. Marie des Hurons

I.S. Joseph

IROQUOIS

Fleuve S. Laurent

Baye de
Niaoure

ANCIEN
PAYS DES
HURONS

LES

LAC ONTARIO

Sault du Fort
Niagara

Onontataret

PAYS DES IROQUOIS

Lac St.
CLAIRE

Riviere Inconnue à tous les Geographes et qu'on
remonte 80 Lieues sans trouver de Saults

Fleuve ou Grand Riviere

Guinashatoua

Village
Missisagues

La P: Pelée

La Longue Pointe

Onontagues

Onnejiouo

LAC ERIE

Toute cette coste n'est presque pas connue

PAYS DES ERIES
Qui ont été détruit par des Iroquois

PENSILVANIE

Village Attigua

Village de Loups Atigua

Village de
Gachimantagem

Philadelphie

NOUVEAU
JERSAY

Chouanon

Baltemore

Darinstonn

Arundelton

Oxfort

Belmbrock

Baye de Laware

Belle Riviere

Village de
Loups

# GEORGIAN BAY:

*the sixth great lake*

# Georgian Bay
## the sixth
## great lake

James P. Barry

1968
CLARKE, IRWIN & COMPANY LIMITED
TORONTO / VANCOUVER

*For my wife ANNE*

*who suffered through the writing of it all*

# Acknowledgements

Much of the research for this book was done in the library of the Ohio Historical Society, at Columbus. Although my subject was alien to the purpose of that library, the staff went far beyond the normal call of duty to help me in every way. The library of the Ohio State University, in Columbus, also holds much Canadian material that I used.

Particular thanks are due the library of the University of Toronto, the library of the University of Western Ontario, and the Toronto Public Library, all of which suggested sources and helped greatly in the work.

The staff of the Public Archives of Canada made a number of suggestions and provided a great deal of material. The staff of the Ontario Provincial Archives was also very helpful.

The Huronia Museum, in Midland, permitted me to go through its extensive collection of old Georgian Bay photographs and to have copies made of some that I needed for further study. The staff of the Collingwood *Enterprise-Bulletin* made its files of historical material available.

Among the individuals who provided information, guidance and encouragement were M. J. Brubacher, W. A. Kennedy, Fred Landon, K. H. Loftus, Ralph K. Rockwood, Jr., B. G. Turner and Richard J. Wright.

Finally I must thank the many people around Georgian Bay who have listened to my foolish questions through the past years and given polite answers.

# Credits

The publishers wish to thank the following organizations for permission to use the photographs acknowledged here.

Canada Steamship Lines Collection of Canadiana, housed at the Manoir Richelieu, Murray Bay, Pointe-au-Bic, P. Que.: The *S.S. Chicora*, The *S.S. Huronic*, The *Nancy*.

Imperial Oil Collection: Etienne Brulé (by C. W. Jefferys).

The Ontario Department of Tourism and Information: Industry on the Bay, Loading timber in Gore Bay, The Martyrs' Shrine, Midland today, Penetanguishene today, A reconstruction of the figurehead of the *Nancy*, A reconstruction of Fort Sainte Marie, Skiing in the Blue Mountains.

The Public Archives of Canada: "Hauling Timber" (by De Rinzy), Samuel de Champlain (by Th. Hamel), "Shooting the Rapids" (by Mrs. F. A. Hopkins).

Toronto Public Libraries: The *Kaloolah* (by C. H. J. Snider), Penetanguishene in 1818.

# Contents

# GEORGIAN BAY:

*the sixth great lake*

# Prologue

Modern geographers are firmly convinced that there are only five Great Lakes: Superior, Michigan, Huron, Erie, and Ontario. But at one time there were six; Captain William Fitzwilliam Owen, Royal Navy, who made the first modern charts of the area in 1815, labelled the large body of water off Lake Huron "Lake Manitoulin." Later this body was decreed to be part of Lake Huron and was named Georgian Bay after George IV. But even now, any traveller in the area will be pointedly corrected if he refers to the Bay as merely an appendage of Lake Huron.

Georgian Bay is impressive enough to be a lake in its own right. Nearly as large as Lake Ontario, it is 120 miles long by 50 miles wide and at the northwestern end it connects with another body of water of similar length, the North Channel. Because the Bay runs from southeast to northwest it is exposed to both the prevailing westerly winds of the Great Lakes and to northerly storms, and the waters can become very rough indeed. From earliest recorded times, small craft have used the inside channel, running along the northeastern shore between the islands and the mainland, to obtain shelter from the waves of the open water.

The western side of the Bay is composed of the limestones of the Niagara escarpment, a rocky spine that passes south of Lake Ontario, swings north across the province of Ontario to form the Bruce Peninsula, continues as Manitoulin Island, and comes to an end in the smaller islands beyond. (The escarpment cliffs and hill masses along the southwestern coast are called the Blue Mountains.) Despite the rugged terrain, both the stretches along the shore and the plateau atop the Blue Mountains are flat and often fertile, and much of this ground has been made into farms.

In contrast, the northeastern shore of the Bay is formed by the bleak rock of the Canadian Shield. Most of the shoreline there is low and only occasionally attains any height. Fringing the shore are the Thirty Thousand Islands, beautiful but treacherous to the navigator.

Between the limestone spine and the southern end of the Thirty Thousand Islands is an irregular sweep of land which provides a string of beaches backed by farms.

A number of rivers flow into the Bay. The Severn, which empties into the southeastern tip, was part of an Indian travel route south to Lake Ontario. The Nottawasaga, which enters on the south shore, was also used to some extent by the Indians but it came into prominence as a waterway during the War of 1812 and the period of pioneer settlement that followed. The French River, which drains into the northeastern corner, is historically the most famous of the Georgian Bay rivers; it was an important waterway in the fur trade days, forming part of the principal canoe route between East and West.

It was by way of the French River that Etienne Brulé in 1610 arrived on Georgian Bay—the first white man to visit the area. The 18-year-old youth had been sent by Champlain, Governor of New France, to learn the customs and language of the Hurons and to explore the region in which they lived. He remained for several years in Huronia and when Champlain himself visited the Bay in 1615 he acted as his interpreter.

Champlain had come to join the Hurons in an expedition against the Iroquois but his allies were slow in mustering. He therefore sent Brulé south to the country of the Andaste Indians who had promised assistance. The young man, with twelve Huron warriors, took what was to become a much-travelled route, by way of Lake Simcoe and the Holland and

Humber Rivers to Lake Ontario. From there he went west to the Niagara River and then struck overland, seeking a course which would lead him safely past the Senecas, the westernmost of the Iroquois tribes. There Brulé disappeared into the forests and Champlain waited in vain for the Andaste reinforcements. The expedition against the Iroquois was a failure, and Champlain, badly wounded, was forced to spend the winter in Huronia.

The following summer, when he was recovered, Champlain went back to Quebec with the Hurons who were making the annual trip to barter furs. He left a message for Brulé, in case he returned, saying that he was to explore the territory to the northwest. Brulé did return, with tales of narrow escapes from death and torture at the hands of the Iroquois. Instead of following Champlain's instructions, however, he rested for a year with the Hurons and then accompanied a party of the Indians to New France.

Sent back to Huronia by Champlain, Brulé continued his explorations and apparently discovered the North Channel. He then returned to New France but the following year, 1621, he was once more back on Georgian Bay, this time with another Frenchman named Grenolle. Together they started out to find the North Sea the Indians had described and were gone for two years. Undoubtedly they went as far as Sault Ste. Marie, and as Brulé later talked about Lake Superior, comparing the Indian report of its length with his own, it is almost certain that he and Grenolle were the first white men to reach this region.

In 1629 Brulé was back in New France which was in the midst of conflict with England. Sent to guide some French ships up the St. Lawrence, he encountered three English vessels under the command of David Kirke and was persuaded to pilot the expedition up the river to Quebec, an act that did not endear him to his countrymen. Quebec was forced to surrender and most of the citizens were taken as prisoners to England. Brulé, however, remained and went back to Huronia where he was murdered, it is said, in a brawl over an Indian woman.

In the meantime, French missionaries had reached Georgian Bay. One of these was Brother Gabriel Sagard, a member of the Récollet order, whose journal still makes amusing reading. Though Sagard was a lay brother, not a priest, he was a well educated man and an observant one. He was, moreover, a relatively unbiased reporter and at times a prophetic one. He feared that contact with civilization would debauch the Indians and that the trade in beaver pelts was contributing to this demoralization. He wrote, "Such a quantity of . . . [pelts] is brought away every year that I cannot think but that the end is in sight."

Sagard had come to Huronia in 1623 with two other missionaries, to convert the Indians, and it troubled him to find that they lacked words to express the concepts of his religion. It was a prospect to discourage the most ambitious missionary. How was he to preach in a language which had no such expressions as *the Kingdom of Heaven* and *the Holy Sacrament*, nor such words as *glory, angels, resurrection, paradise, church, temptation, hell, faith, hope,* and *charity*? He commented sadly that there was no need there for learned clergymen, but a great one for men who feared God and were patient and full of love.

When spring came the Hurons made ready for the yearly trading expedition to the French colonies. By this time the missionaries needed supplies, and Brother Sagard was one of those selected to make the trip to New France. As he was preparing to leave, his Huron friends came to see him. Some mourned his departure, for they feared that he might never return; some asked him to bring various trinkets for them; others asked him to tell the fur traders at Quebec of the fair treatment he had received and ask them to deal fairly with the Hurons in return.

In Quebec Sagard gathered his supplies and transacted his business in fairly short order. He was about to leave once more for Huronia when he received a letter from the Father Provincial of the Récollets, ordering him to return to France by the next ship. The Indians had predicted truly.

# Huron harvest

*Bearded canoemen checked the priming of their muskets or fingered their tomahawks. The one small cannon was loaded and ready. Between prayers the Father Superior joined his men on the wall, to look to the east, where a few miles away the flames and smoke of a burning village rose into the sky.*

*It was March 16, 1649. The mission fort of Sainte Marie, on the eastern shore of Georgian Bay, was prepared for attack. A thousand hostile Iroquois warriors swarmed over the nearby villages of the friendly Huron Indians. The stone walls and log palisades of the little fort sheltered about fifty Frenchmen. This was the westernmost post of New France, hundreds of miles to the west of any English or Dutch settlement, and a tortuous thirty-day canoe trip from Quebec in midsummer. In March the lakes and rivers were impassable to French canoes. There was no possibility of reinforcement. If the governor at Quebec knew of this attack—which he did not—and had troops to spare—which he did not—there was no way of getting them to Sainte Marie.*

*So the Frenchmen stood by their weapons and said their prayers. They kept their eyes fixed on the trail that came from the burning village. They thought of what must be happening to Father Jean de Brébeuf and his young companion Gabriel Lalemant, who had been captured there; and they renewed their prayers.*

In the early seventeenth century, 30,000 Huron Indians lived in a peninsula 25 miles long by 50 miles wide, along the south-eastern shore of Georgian Bay. Their country was compact and strategically located. They traded with other nations to the west across the Great Lakes and to the east along the French River-Lake Nipissing-Ottawa River-Saint Lawrence River route. In the east they traded more and more as the years passed with the French, who gave porcelain beads and metal implements in return for beaver pelts.

The French commander was Samuel de Champlain, a man who combined vision, practical ability, and persistence. He persisted until his aims became the colonial policies of France, and until he was made governor of New France. And he worked ceaselessly at his interlocking purposes: Christian-ization of the Indians of North America, exploration of the continent with the hope of finding a passage to the Orient, and trade.

The Hurons were constantly at war with the Iroquois Fed-eration of Five Nations, which lived in what now is upstate New York. Their wars early in that century consisted largely of raids, in which a small band from one nation would descend on an unsuspecting hunting or fishing party from the other and try to carry off prisoners; captured women and children would be adopted into the tribe and captured warriors would often be tortured to death. It was a sport, a mixture of a hunt and a game between competing teams, but it also sometimes was used for the classic purpose of war, to extend political action.

As Huron trade with the French increased, Iroquois raids increased. The French-Huron combination may have seemed potentially dangerous to the Iroquois who therefore wanted to block its growth. Moreover, the Hurons carried in their canoes trade goods which the Iroquois could use. As a result of these attacks, the Hurons asked Champlain to help them in an expedition against the Iroquois.

The expedition was a failure. The Hurons furnished 500 instead of the 2,500 warriors they had promised. When the Huron army reached the Iroquois village that was its objective, it disintegrated into a wild mob, which Champlain could not control, and was driven off by the defenders.

After that one trip, Champlain never returned to Huronia. He spent the rest of his days in Quebec or in France, struggling with merchants and politicians for the life of his colony. But he sent able men to do his work. Father LeCaron, who had accompanied Champlain on his trip, returned to the Hurons with two other Récollets for a year in 1623. Jean Nicolet, a young man whom Champlain had sent to live with the Indians, set out at the governor's wish, to reach Cathay by way of the Great Lakes, and eventually landed on the oriental shore now called Wisconsin. Finally, Champlain sent to the Huron country the Jesuit missionary, Jean de Brébeuf. Officially Brébeuf reported to his religious superiors, but he also combined the offices of ambassador and viceroy, carrying out Champlain's policies.

Brébeuf was a giant from seventeenth century Europe who had been transplanted to the North American wilderness. His religious thought was of a kind that might startle the most devout person today. He saw visions in the north woods: a demon in the shape of a woman tempted him, and when he spurned it, it disappeared; and once with grimly accurate prophecy he saw a cross approaching from the Iroquois country, "Big enough," as he told his companions, "to crucify us all."

Brébeuf was also master of American Indian languages and a student of Indian customs. Archaeologists today read his reports to learn what the Huron Indians were like, and use his descriptions to locate Huron burial places accurately. Few white men have better understood Indian psychology or have entered into Indian politics with more finesse. And few men dedicated to a cause have been less assuming than this enormous priest who was not above referring to himself as an ox, punning on his own name.

In 1626, when he was thirty-three years old, Brébeuf first made plans to start westward from Quebec, but the Indians looked at this great, black-robed man, and flatly refused to take him; his imposing size and his dress made them suspicious. Probably he was a magician. All they said, however, was that he was too big for the bark canoes. He summoned all of his growing skill at Indian oratory and finally, after considerable

9

talk diplomatically punctuated with a great many presents of beads and trinkets, he persuaded them to take him.

With him went another Jesuit and a Récollet friar. Neither of the other missionaries stayed long in the isolated wilderness of the Huron country, but Brébeuf remained alone until he was called back to New France in 1629. He arrived there just in time to be captured in the English victory following the first siege of Quebec, and to be carried off to England as a prisoner. Later he was permitted to go to France; and as Canada had been returned to France by treaty, he was soon on a ship bound westward.

Once more in Quebec, he wanted to return to Huronia. Again the Indians were cool; it was a year before satisfactory arrangements could be made with the Hurons who came to the French colony to trade. By that time the Hurons were suffering from a violent epidemic of smallpox, one of the first of those white man's diseases that were to plague the American Indian for the next three hundred years. Undaunted, Brébeuf once more used the diplomatic approach, doubled the number of gifts, and was soon on his way. In his party were several other Frenchmen, each of whom rode alone in a canoe manned by very sick Indians.

The long journey up the Ottawa River, across country to Lake Nipissing, and down French River to Georgian Bay was never a pleasure trip. Brébeuf recorded matter-of-factly that there were thirty-five portages, some of them six miles long, and at least fifty places where they had to get out of the canoes and pull them upstream through the rapids. But now, in addition to the usual hazards of the trip, they faced sick Indians who were surly and mean. The canoemen marooned some of the passengers along the way and paddled off and left them. They robbed others of all they carried. The French were forced to paddle most of the way and to carry full loads on portages; it was killing work for untrained men.

After he was established in Huronia, however, Brébeuf settled down to one of the few quiet periods he was to enjoy during the rest of his life. The Jesuits had an Indian long house, made of bark over a frame of bent saplings, which they had converted to their living quarters and chapel. Their simple furnishings captivated the Hurons, who came to marvel at such things as a small hand mill for grinding corn, or carpenter-made doors, built by the French workmen who had accompanied the priests.

One of the Frenchmen noticed a group of Hurons one day gazing in awe at the clock on the wall. They called it the Chief of the Day, and were sure that it was alive. So the Frenchman told them that when the clock struck four in the afternoon, the Chief was saying, "Go away, go out so that we can close the door," and that when it struck noon he was saying, "Put the kettle on the fire." After that the Hurons invariably took the hint and left at four o'clock; but at noon the usual group of visitors was joined by crowds of hungry Indians looking for a hand-out. Amused, Brébeuf found room to put the story in his yearly report, sandwiched between earnest theological discussions and careful descriptions of Huron customs.

The missionaries saw constant signs of the guerilla warfare between Iroquois and Hurons. At one point Brébeuf managed to convert a captive Iroquois warrior. He baptized him before the Hurons tortured him to death, and he tried to help him in his last hours. Father LeMercier, one of those present, wrote: "We recommended his soul to God, and returned home to say Mass. We would, indeed, have desired to prevent this act of lawlessness; but it is not yet in our power. We are not the masters here. It is not a trifling thing to have a whole country opposed to one—a barbarous country too, such as this is."

The main purpose of the missionaries was to convert the Indians. Sometimes they worked for days with natives who would accept any belief in order to win the friendship of a man who had some tobacco, but who would speedily forget the belief after he gave them the tobacco. Some Hurons were sufficiently impressed to remember the sermons for a time, but few, in the priests' opinion, were earnest enough to merit baptism.

Much of the Jesuits' energy also went towards fighting the smallpox epidemics which struck the Indians again and again. The missionaries could not understand why smallpox appeared in exactly those places where they went; they did not realize that they were the carriers of the disease. As the epidemics killed more Hurons, the missionaries drew more blame. The natural suspicion the Indians had for strange people, clothing, and religious ceremonies was increased by whispering campaigns started by the medicine men who were, of course, violently opposed to Jesuit ideas. Several times the missionaries were summoned to councils, where the wise men and chiefs gathered to pass judgement on them for making the black magic that brought disease. Each time Brébeuf's understanding of the Indian language and the Indian mind saved them. He was able to out-argue the most determined Huron. On one occasion the meeting went on far into the night, till one by one the Indians grew tired and fell asleep or wandered away. An old man, as he left, told Brébeuf, "If they decide to split your head, we won't say a word." But the missionary held his ground until no one was left to make that decision.

One day a friendly Huron came to the Jesuits in panic, to say that a council had just met and had condemned them to death. Immediately they went to the meeting, with Brébeuf in the lead, and faced the chiefs. For a time the lives of the Frenchmen hung in the balance. But the Hurons were not able to withstand French eloquence. When the chiefs spoke, it was not to announce a death sentence; instead, they said that they wanted to call a grand council of the entire country, to consider the problem. Brébeuf answered that he would be glad to meet with such a council.

He returned to the bark long house and wrote a will, which he intended to leave with some Christian Hurons to be delivered to Quebec if the Jesuits all were killed. In it he said that if any of the priests or their French servants were left alive they were going to take shelter in the houses of their best friends among the Indians. They would give the equipment of their chapel to their most vigorous convert for safekeeping. And they would take special care to put in a safe place their Huron dictionary and the other records of the Huron language which they had compiled over the years with much effort.

To show the Hurons then how little he cared for life on earth, Brébeuf gave a farewell feast, such as a dying Indian or a condemned prisoner might give. He invited all the people of the neighborhood. In awe and astonishment they came, crowding into the Jesuit's house, and enjoyed themselves. After that the general assembly to condemn the missionaries was never called.

When Samuel de Champlain died at Quebec on Christmas Day, 1635, he had accomplished much. He had founded the colony of Quebec and had protected it from its enemies both in France and along the St. Lawrence; he had sent explorers thousands of miles westward to investigate the lands and peoples there; he had encouraged the Hurons to build up a trading empire which brought pelts from as far away as Lake Superior and Hudson Bay and funnelled them into New France. And the priests he had sent to work among the Hurons had made progress that was slow but measurable. In the summer of 1636, Champlain's successor arrived in the colony. The new governor and his lieutenant, dressed in the robes of the Knights of Malta, moved with a uniformed retinue from the river bank to the fort. As he and his staff proceeded towards the church, they passed a crucifix by the roadside and fell to their knees to pray. Charles Huault de Montmagny had been educated by the Society of Jesus, and clerical historians alike assure us that he was a good man. He governed the colony for the greater glory of God. Missions were of primary importance. Exploration and trade were useful if they expanded the mission field. The balanced vision of Champlain was replaced by the missionary fervor of a man who saw a heathen continent awaiting conversion.

The changes at Quebec did not at first affect Huronia. Brébeuf, now working to found a second establishment there, wrote, ". . . we have good hope of some day reaping a large harvest of souls at this mission." But in 1638 Father Jerome Lalemant arrived in Huronia, at the end of a long and difficult journey from France. He took office as Superior of the Huron missions. Brébeuf remained as a subordinate. The difference between the two men was striking. Brébeuf was a master of Indian languages and politics with many years of experience among the Indians; Lalemant was an unyielding zealot with little knowledge of the new world. To him the Huron country was a stronghold of demons. Every Huron custom was inspired by the Devil. He was unable to see that

13

European ideals could not be applied to the Indians, and he insisted that native converts remain aloof from the life of their people.

Lalemant also won the enmity of the tribesmen by interfering with their ceremonies. It was a custom of the Hurons each year to choose two young virgins to be married to the god of the fish nets, a symbolic rite intended to produce a more fertile catch. Brébeuf, in describing it, made the wry comment that he was glad to see Hurons honoring virginity in some way. But after Lalemant's accession, the Jesuits intervened to stop the custom and aroused the extreme indignation of the Indians.

Under Father Lalemant's command, the missionaries did their work more vigorously. At the same time, Huron distrust of them grew. The Jesuits went farther afield, to outlying villages and then to more distant tribes, to spread the gospel. Wherever they went, the recurring epidemics of smallpox appeared.

Partly because of the increasing hostility of the Indians around them and partly because the growing missions needed a central headquarters, Lalemant soon decided to establish a residence away from any Huron village but in the centre of the country. He chose a site on the river now called the Wye and had an Indian long house built there. He named the new residence Sainte Marie.

At this time the Iroquois to the south had almost exterminated the fur-bearing animals in their own country. By 1640 they found themselves in a desperate situation. Without pelts they were unable to get from the Dutch the trade articles that had become necessities. If they could not obtain iron axes and metal tools, they could not compete for long with other tribes supplied by the French, the Swedes, and for that matter, the Dutch.

The warlike Iroquois did not have to look far to see an answer to their problem. The Huron trading empire was functioning well; each year Huron canoes took bales of furs to New France and loads of trade goods back again. Disease had killed two-thirds of the Huron population since the Frenchmen's first arrival, so there were not a great many warriors to protect this wealth. Furthermore, despite feeble efforts of the New Netherlands government to control the weapons, Dutch traders had supplied the Iroquois with muskets. The French colonial government, on the other hand, firmly refused to arm any Huron who was not a thoroughgoing Christian.

Throughout 1641 and 1642 Huron spies brought rumours of an attack which was coming from the Iroquois country. In 1642 a Huron village was struck by an Iroquois force and burned. That same year one of the many Iroquois parties which lay in ambush along the Ottawa and St. Lawrence to attack the Hurons and steal their goods, intercepted larger game. Twelve canoes, carrying the year's supplies to the Huron mission in the care of Father Isaac Jogues and two French assistants, paddled into ambush. The prisoners and booty were carried away to the Iroquois country.

Raids continued. Sixty Hurons Quebec-bound with furs were ambushed at Montreal the next spring. Four fleets of canoes left Huronia for New France in 1644; only one made the round trip. The French of course tried to fight off the attacks. In 1640 Father Lalemant wrote from Huronia, asking Cardinal Richelieu for help. In 1641 Father LeJeune, a former Superior of the Quebec missions, was sent to France by the governor to get assistance for the colony. In 1642 material and men to build a fort on the approaches to Quebec, at the mouth of the River Richelieu, arrived from France, and at about the same time Father LeJeune wrote that Cardinal Richelieu had made a sizable grant of money to build a fort in the Huron country. In 1644 twenty-two soldiers from France were sent on to Huronia and probably spent the winter building the fort, at the mission headquarters, Sainte Marie. Unfortunately they returned to New France the next summer and no comparable force was ever garrisoned in Huronia again.

In 1644 Father Jerome Lalemant was promoted from Superior of the Huron Missions to Superior of Canada, at Quebec, where he would have a strong voice in all of the affairs of New France. Lalemant left behind him some Hurons who were reported to be outstanding Christians. He also left a split in the Huron nation. Christian Hurons were fed in time of famine and were given fire-arms; they were permitted to enter the base at Sainte Marie; they were encouraged to exercise their consciences not only upon themselves but also upon their erring neighbours. The results of all this were illustrated when a Huron war party was defeated by a force one sixth its size; the Christian Hurons in it had been indignantly praying for defeat because their leader had consulted a magician before battle.

Father Ragueneau, who had spent some years in Huronia, followed Father Lalemant as Superior. He was a moderate person, who didn't see devils behind every bush. Under his direction the missionaries were more understanding, and although distrust still existed between Indians and Frenchmen, the Hurons became more friendly. Brébeuf, judging from his letters, thoroughly approved of Ragueneau.

Brébeuf now became dean of the missionaries, the first of the men at Sainte Marie to have reached Huronia. It was natural that when the young priest Gabriel Lalemant, nephew of the recently promoted Superior of Canada, arrived in the country, he would first be sent out with Brébeuf to serve an apprenticeship in his missionary duties.

Iroquois attacks continued; in 1648 Father Daniel was killed when an Iroquois war party captured a Huron village. The Hurons were building a new village named St. Ignace, five miles away from Sainte Marie, and they asked Brébeuf to help lay it out and to design an effective system of palisades to protect it.

St. Ignace was almost completed in the late winter of 1649, and about 400 Hurons were living there. When the invading army of a thousand Iroquois reached the Huron country that March, St. Ignace was directly in its path. Iroquois scouts crept along the walls at night and found one place where the stockade had not been completed; the builders had left a gap so that they still could draw logs into the town. At dawn the enemy poured in through the opening, surprising the people of the village so completely that only three of them escaped.

The three villagers fled across the snow to the neighbouring mission village of St. Louis, where Brébeuf and young Gabriel Lalemant were staying, and gave the alarm. There was wild activity in St. Louis. Warriors ran to the walls. Women quickly gathered up their children and a few belongings and hurried away towards the interior of the country. As the women, children, and old men streamed out of the town, the Hurons urged the priests to go too, but they refused.

The Iroquois reached St. Louis before sunrise. They attacked. The sound of their musket fire mingled with yells and screams. The eighty Hurons who were left in the village beat off the assault. They knew that the penalty for defeat in Indian warfare was quick death if they were lucky and torture if they were not. The Iroquois attacked again. The defenders threw rocks down on them and tomahawked those who reached the top. The Iroquois fell back, then rallied and came on again. Instead of trying to scale the walls this time, they attacked the wooden palisade with axes, cutting away the logs and undermining the wall. Then they pushed through the breach and in hand-to-hand fighting overwhelmed the Hurons.

The two missionaries were prize captives. With a few of the Huron survivors, they were taken back to St. Ignace. To the Iroquois they were powerful French chiefs, and they received the treatment due their rank. Descriptions of their tortures came from Huron witnesses who managed to escape during the orgy that followed and from Frenchmen who examined their bodies afterward. They were exposed to the full range of savage ingenuity but both men died bravely.

Huron war parties tried to push the Iroquois back and failed. The gutted town of St. Louis, where Brébeuf and Lalemant had been captured, was occupied and reoccupied several times, first by one side and then by the other. Wounded Hurons sought refuge inside the walls of Sainte Marie and Iroquois scouts prowled outside, but the French base was never attacked.

Fort Sainte Marie stood, but the Huron nation collapsed around it. The great Iroquois attack that caused the deaths of Brébeuf and Gabriel Lalemant was also the death blow of the Hurons as a people. They deserted their country and went to live with other tribes or hid in remote places. Many of them went farther west. Only one group stayed on; it moved to a large island a short distance from the Huron shore, now called Christian Island. The Jesuits went there also, to be with the

Indians, burning Sainte Marie behind them to keep it from becoming an Iroquois stronghold.

The small Huron remnant suffered starvation and disease during the next winter. Indians who tried to leave the island to hunt or fish were pounced upon by roving Iroquois bands. Those who did not leave it were driven to eating the bodies of their dead relatives. Finally, in the spring of 1650, two of the older chiefs called upon the Father Superior secretly and told him that the Hurons had decided to leave the island. They had various plans: to live alone in the forest, to go a six days' journey farther away from the Iroquois, to go to friendly tribes, or even to join the enemy, among whom they had friends and relatives who urged them to act before it was too late. But the chiefs asked the Jesuits instead to take the Hurons with them to some place in New France.

Father Ragueneau reported the conference to the other Jesuits. They deliberated for some time and prayed for guidance. The vision of a Christian nation, living peacefully on the shore of the western lakes, was hard to abandon. But finally they decided that the only way to save the people and to insure their continued adherence to the faith was to move them to a fort near Quebec.

On the tenth of June the sad remnants of the tribe paddled away from their country. "Amid these regrets the thought was consoling that we were to take away with us poor Christian families numbering about three hundred souls," Ragueneau commented.

The vision of a Christian nation on the shores of Georgian Bay was not fulfilled, but Huronia still had played an important part in the exploration of North America. It had served as a base for travellers ranging in character from the distinguished Champlain to the notorious Brulé. It had provided material for both missionary and secular reports that were published in France and that gave people there an interest in the further development of the new world.

# Highway to the west

After the dispersal of the Hurons, the French used the Bay as a highway for westward exploration and trade. It was the era of Groseilliers, Radisson, and their equally intrepid, although lesser-known successors.

In 1658 the adventurer-trader Groseilliers, who for a time in the 1640's had been a lay assistant in the Huron missions, set out on a journey to the west, accompanied by his young brother-in-law Radisson and a large group of Huron and Ottawa Indians. They crossed rapid and portage until they reached a bay of clear water, full of rocks, small isles, and an infinite number of fishes and otters. It was Georgian Bay.

When they came to the Bay, the Indians separated into two parties, the Ottawas going directly to the northwest, the Hurons turning south, apparently in order to pass by their old homeland. The Frenchmen saw from a distance the site of the former Jesuit mission and noted the many open fields where the Hurons had once lived. Then the group proceeded northwest, visited an Indian village on a large island—probably the Ottawa village on Manitoulin Island—and went on through the Straits of Mackinac to southern Wisconsin, where they spent the winter.

In the spring of 1659 the two explorers travelled a considerable distance to the south and probably became the first white men to see the upper Mississippi River. In the spring of 1660 they turned north again, to an island in the upper Mississippi where a village of Huron refugees was located. From the Indians the adventurers received a large quantity of beaver pelts, and prepared an expedition to return to New France. Just as they were ready to leave, word came that the Iroquois were again barring the way. The Hurons immediately wanted to cancel the voyage, but Radisson and Groseilliers asked for a council to be called.

Over eight hundred Indians gathered. They sat on the ground in a circle about the two men. Groseilliers spoke first. He asked if the Frenchmen were the friends of the Hurons or of their enemies. Did the Hurons intend to wait for the Iroquois to come for them and take them like beavers in traps? If they had no courage how could they defend their wives and children? Groseilliers then turned to Radisson. The beardless young man stood up. He seized a beaver skin robe worn by one of the Indians and beat him with it, asking if that was how they intended to fight. He fought with arms, not robes. If the Hurons would not face the Iroquois, why should the French come to them again, he asked—to baptize the dead? How did the Hurons expect to live without French trade? For their part, the two Frenchmen would rather die like men than live like beggars. At that point the two of them turned and walked out of the gathering, leaving the Indians speechless.

Soon afterwards the Hurons announced that they would go to New France. The expedition set out, five hundred strong. They passed through the Great Lakes, up the French River, and down the Ottawa. Although they had some skirmishes with Iroquois, the two traders managed to sustain the nerve of their followers, and the enemy Indians were driven off. The flotilla of canoes passed on downstream. When Radisson and Groseilliers finally arrived at the city of Quebec they were saluted by the guns of the fort and by those of the three ships in harbour—ships which, except for them, would have had to return to France without a cargo of furs.

Having been so successful, the partners planned another voyage to the west in 1661. The Governor of the colony announced that they must take along two of his men, who would share in the profits. Radisson and Groseilliers objected strongly: "We made the governor a slight answer and told him for our part we knowed what we were: discoverers before governors; we should be glad to have the honour of his company, but not that of his servants, and that we were both masters and servants." The Governor was not pleased. He gave orders that they could not go until they had his permission. Soon afterwards they left by night.

During the next year and a half Radisson and Groseilliers penetrated westward to the Sioux country and probably travelled north to Hudson Bay. They learned of the routes to the Bay and conceived a plan that in time would revolutionize the Canadian fur trade. They reasoned that ships coming into Hudson Bay could bring in trade goods and carry out furs, that the distance from there to the tribes around Lake Superior was much shorter than the long, difficult canoe trip from Quebec, that no Iroquois blocked the routes between Hudson Bay and the Great Lakes, and that any traders who came that way would thus have great advantages.

In 1663 the two men once more returned to New France, with over 300 canoes full of furs. Once more they had saved the colony from imminent financial ruin. They hoped to be greeted as heroes. Instead the Governor, who remembered the manner of their departure, threw Groseilliers into jail. Then he fined the partners four thousand pounds, ostensibly to build a fort at Three Rivers. He fined them an additional six thousand pounds "for the country," which went directly into his own pocket. And he levied a customs charge of one-fourth, an additional fourteen thousand pounds.

Once Groseilliers was out of prison, the two partners took their grievances to France, seeking justice, but found none. Eventually they made their way to England with their scheme of trading by ship into Hudson Bay. In London they met rich men willing to back them, and the Hudson's Bay Company was formed.

As the French brought more force to bear against the Iroquois and were able to explore Lake Ontario, the route from the present site of Toronto to Georgian Bay via the

Humber River, a portage, Lake Simcoe, and some of the connecting streams also came into use. Jean Perret used it in 1669 and is sometimes credited with discovering it. La Salle passed over it on one of his trips in 1680. Although the French River approach to the Bay was still the more common one, both were undoubtedly used often by others travelling to and from the west, many of them men whose journeys were not recorded.

During this time the lower Great Lakes also came into use as an alternate route. By 1679 La Salle had launched the first ship above Niagara Falls, the *Griffin*, and she had sailed from her building place through Erie and Huron. Unfortunately the bad luck that dogged La Salle struck also at his ship. She disappeared with her grumbling crew on the return voyage— possibly scuttled or wrecked at the entrance to Georgian Bay —and the French built no more ships on the Lakes west of Ontario. Until the British took over, cargoes and men went westward only in canoes or small boats. As a result, the comparatively sheltered routes leading through Georgian Bay offered many advantages over the open waters of Lake Erie and Lake Huron.

In 1749 the French built a small fort on Lake Ontario, directly south of Georgian Bay. Fort Rouillé, the forerunner of Toronto, was built to control the passage between Georgian Bay and Lake Ontario, to stop the Indians who tried to go on to trade with the British at Oswego, and to block English traders who wanted to go north. The route itself was at first called the Toronto Portage, until it became common practice to refer to the southern end of the passage as Toronto. By 1757 the name was applied in some of the records to the fort on Lake Ontario.

The fight for North America between France and England did not reach into the Upper Lakes, but when it was over the results soon became evident there. The French had made much effort to understand the Indians and to persuade them through politic leadership to do what Frenchmen desired. The insistence of the Church that each Indian had a soul to be saved was a strong reason for this relationship, but the French attitude went beyond that. Traders who despised the missionaries dealt easily with the Indians. The *coureurs de bois* lived among them, and with their women, and in many ways came to think like them. There was more rapport between white men and red during the French time than ever afterwards. Most of the British, on the other hand, were prone to think of Indians as naked savages of decidedly inferior type. General Amherst, the bluff administrator who took over direction of Indian affairs for the British Crown, shared these views.

The restless tribes had no peace treaties with the British and they thought that the French might return at any time, an expectation that was encouraged by some of the Frenchmen who still travelled among them. If the English king wanted their friendship he should make the proper ceremonial overtures. Amherst, for his part, stoutly ordered that no presents be given the tribesmen and in every way treated them summarily. In 1763 the Indian nations rose in what became known as Pontiac's War, overwhelmed Mackinac and all of the other western forts except Detroit, Niagara, and Fort Pitt, and killed most of the defenders.

Military action and economic pressure brought the war to an end. The colonies mustered their full strength. The Indian nations desperately needed trade goods—they no longer could survive without gunpowder, for example—and as a result of the fighting they were effectively blockaded. The war ended in a series of councils and treaties. By September of 1764 Mackinac was reoccupied.

Albany and Montreal now competed as headquarters for the British fur trade. The Albany traders used the Toronto Portage to reach the northwest through Georgian Bay, but Montreal soon won easily. No one could do without the Frenchmen. Often they were the only ones who could approach the Indians. They knew the routes, the business methods, and the equipment. Thus the new British trade looked much like the old French trade. The same canoes passed over the same routes, particularly the Ottawa River—French River passage to Georgian Bay and through the Bay to the west.

One of the first English colonists to enter the trade was a native of New Jersey, Alexander Henry. At first he took a

French partner to guide him and to deal with the Indians. He made his base at Montreal, and in 1761 came down French River to Georgian Bay, camping at the mouth of the river in order to repair his canoes. There was a south wind, the waves ran high, and breakers crashed on the rocks. Henry was at first alarmed when his companions set out over the rough water, but he soon found that the canoes rode easily on the waves.

Henry and his party coasted along the shore, heading north and west, past Point aux Grondines—Grumbling Point—which gains its name from the constant noise of water among the rocks. Next day they came to the island of La Cloche, so called because a rock there, when struck, rang like a bell. On the island was a large village of Indians, who were quite friendly until they discovered that Henry was English, not French, and their manner changed. Henry, they said, would certainly be killed at Mackinac when the Indians there learned that he was an Englishman, and his goods would be taken. That of course would be unfair to the La Cloche Indians, who should have a share of the loot. Therefore if Henry cared to contribute a keg of rum they would be very pleased; if he did not, they would take it anyway.

Henry made the contribution and the Indians at La Cloche molested him no more, but because of their constant warnings that he surely would be killed at Mackinac, he decided to take the precaution of dressing like a French trader. He put on "a cloth passed about the middle, a shirt hanging loose, a molton, or blanket coat, and a large, red, milled worsted cap." Then he smeared his face and hands with grease and dirt, and when they left La Cloche he took his place as one of the canoemen. Whenever Indians appeared he bent to the paddle with as much skill as he could muster. In this way he proceeded to Mackinac, where his disguise was at first successful, until some of his men gave away his identity to the Indians. Luckily, British troops arrived to garrison the fort before any real harm could come to him.

During the next ten years Alexander Henry became one of the most successful traders on the Great Lakes. In 1775 he decided to move on to join the growing body of men who were

24

tapping the wealth of Saskatchewan. He went with Peter Pond, another adventurer, and joined the two Frobishers en route. They made an informal agreement to coordinate their efforts that season, and thus formed the embryo of the future North West Company, giant of the Montreal fur trade.

The *voyageur* was the backbone of the Montreal fur empire. This small, cheerful, tough man with a brightly coloured sash and shirt came from the banks of the St. Lawrence between Three Rivers and Montreal. His forebears may well have been *coureurs de bois*—independent traders in the tradition of Radisson and Groseilliers—but as the big companies grew, there became less and less room for individual trading efforts. The *voyageur* was a canoeman in the service of one of the trading companies. He made little money, but he enjoyed adventure, travel, and escape from a dull life, the things that traditionally caused men to become sailors.

His job was to move trade goods from Montreal to the farthest posts and to return with furs from the distant interior to Montreal, all between the spring break-up of ice in the rivers and lakes and the last freeze of autumn. This was done in relays, with brigades of big *canôts du maître* operating between Montreal and Grand Portage, at the head of Lake Superior, and smaller *canôts du nord* from Grand Portage westward. The *voyageur* worked constantly against time, with the vision of winter pursuing him. He slept perhaps five hours, rose at three in the morning, and paddled hours before breakfast. Throughout the day his only respite was the five or ten minute break each hour during which he puffed on his long clay pipe. After supper (dried peas, pork, and seabiscuit westward bound; corn mixed with lard or bear fat on the return trip), at nine or ten at night, he promptly went to sleep, his head and shoulders under the protection of an upturned canoe. Next morning he rushed on again.

By the middle of May the canoe brigades from Montreal were leaving Lake Nipissing and starting down the French River. At that point, with ceremony, the *voyageurs* threw away their setting poles—the long, slim, metal-shod poles used to push the canoes up stretches of quick-flowing water—and paddled down the river, singing as they came. There still were five portages to cross. All were relatively short, however, the longest being the Parisienne, of a hundred paces. As they came to each portage, the men jumped out into waist-deep water so that the fragile canoes would not touch land, and quickly began to unload. They crossed these carries at a trot, with at least two ninety-pound packs on each of their backs, held by tump-lines across their foreheads, and then returned to carry more. But as they reached Georgian Bay the *voyageurs* left behind them the killing portages. From the mouth of the French River to Sault Ste. Marie, the *voyageurs* had only to paddle, their greatest risk being the storms which sometimes forced a brigade to camp on a nearby island until danger had passed.

One of the brigades that entered the Bay in spring and went back through it in fall consisted of from three to (in later years) ten big, brightly-decorated canoes, each laden with some three tons of cargo and paddled by ten or twelve men. In charge of the brigade was the Guide, who had worked up through the ranks, and who stood in the bow of the first canoe and chose the way. He had the same authority and responsibility for his canoes and men that the master of a ship had for his ship and sailors. In a big brigade he might have a second, less-experienced guide to assist him.

At various times North West Company repair stations were set up at Little Current and at the mouth of the Mississagi River, where they could take care of any serious damage that occurred on the difficult route from Montreal. The most permanent station in these waters was Fort La Cloche, built by the North West Company about 1790 on La Cloche Island. The fort, consisting of one or two large log buildings and a little village of huts, stood near the juncture of Georgian Bay proper and the North Channel, roughly at the midway point between Montreal and the head of Lake Superior, a logical place for a repair and service station. In addition, it served as a trading post for local Indians.

The Montreal traders were also acutely interested in other routes. A second artery of trade in the British era ran up the St. Lawrence River, through Lake Ontario, over the Niagara Portage to Lake Erie, and thence to Detroit or Mackinac.

Goods were carried in *bateaux*, in the government vessels of the Provincial Marine, and after 1785, when the ban on private vessels was lifted, in commercial sailing vessels. It was less expensive to send goods this way, but also much slower, a great disadvantage in a business that depended on rapid transport.

The Treaty of Paris, between Britain and the new United States, gave the south shore of the Great Lakes to the Americans. Britain ignored this part of the treaty for some years, but the Nor'Westers seem to have thought about the day when the United States might really gain that southern shore. The year after the North West Company was formed, Frobisher and McTavish of the Company were at Mackinac, conferring with military authorities on the use of the Toronto Passage. In 1785 Benjamin Frobisher urged the improvement of that route to add security to the frontier.

In 1794 the Americans, by military and diplomatic effort, won the south shore of the Great Lakes; the entire southern flank of the British line of communications westward and of the fur trading route was thus occupied by the United States. Suddenly the Toronto Portage became critically important. Governor Simcoe not only moved his seat of government away from Niagara, at the border, to the new village of York he had had begun the previous year at the site of Toronto, but he also set to work to extend a main street of that village to Lake Simcoe (which he named for his father), to a point from which cargoes and men could be moved by water to Georgian Bay and through it to the west. Yonge Street was extended along the old Indian trail, using troop labour. It remained a vital road during the years that followed.

Once the United States was established on the Great Lakes shore it made its presence felt. The North West Company and other Montreal traders complained of the vexatious interference with their boats and property by the American customs officials at Niagara in 1796 and the years following. In 1799 the North West Company gave £12,000 towards the improvement of Yonge Street. In 1808 a group of merchants objected strongly because the American customs officer at Niagara had seized eight of their *bateaux*; use of the Toronto route continued to grow under such pressure. By 1811 the

North West Company proposed a further road from Lake Simcoe to Penetanguishene on Georgian Bay in order to shorten the complex water route between the two bodies of water and asked for a grant of 2,000 acres at each end, offering to pay £4,000 in goods to the Indians. The first survey of the road was completed in August of 1812.

# 1812

In 1812 the United States declared war. Events on the Upper Lakes at first favoured the British, who took Mackinac and Detroit. But in September of 1813 Commodore Perry won an American victory on Lake Erie, and the British commander General Procter abandoned Detroit, and was defeated in the Battle of the Thames by the American leader General Harrison.

As the result of these British defeats, the fort at Mackinac was vulnerable. American ships had merely to sail up Lake Huron and attack it. However, Perry's fleet needed to refit after the battle, and then autumn was at hand. If the ships went out then, they stood a chance of being frozen in the ice all winter. The attack was therefore delayed until the next spring.

The peril of Mackinac was as evident to the British as it was to the Americans. Supplies for the post were sent across the Toronto Passage late in 1813, but the boats carrying them froze in the ice of Lake Simcoe. The officer in charge, one Commissary Crookshank, reported in January to General Drummond, British commander in Upper Canada, that it was not practical to open the road to Penetanguishene in mid-winter and with the resources at his disposal, but that a portage could be opened to the Nottawasaga River, which flows into Georgian Bay. Drummond approved.

In February a sizable force left Kingston to go to Mackinac via the Nottawasaga. It was commanded by Lt. Col. Robert McDouall of the Glengarry Light Infantry and consisted of a party of shipwrights, twenty-one seamen, eleven artillerymen in charge of four field guns, and two companies of the Royal Newfoundland Regiment. They went to York, which still was recovering from its capture and brief occupation by the Americans the preceding spring, and thence north over Yonge Street, Lake Simcoe, and the portage to the Nottawasaga. They reached the river about thirty miles from its outlet, built huts to shelter themselves from the Canadian winter, and set to work constructing thirty large *bateaux*, using wood cut on the spot.

*Bateau*, of course, simply means boat. From colonial times on, however, the name was applied to a particular kind of boat used generally on the western lakes. It was a flat-bottomed, double-ended craft intended to be propelled mainly by oars or poles, although at times sails were also used. It may be surmised that the ones built on the Nottawasaga were fairly crude when one considers the conditions under which they were assembled.

In April the *bateaux* were loaded with supplies for Mackinac; the men broke the ice on the upper reaches of the river and began to move the boats towards its mouth. After working their way for several days to the shore of the Bay, McDouall's group started across the open water, picking a course through the ice fields. For nineteen days they moved across Georgian Bay and Lake Huron, struggling through the floating ice and constant storms. Only one boat was lost, and its crew and cargo were saved. On May 18th they arrived at Mackinac Island and McDouall assumed command of all British forces there.

The American expedition to clear the British from Lake Huron moved slowly. First there were arguments about who was to command it; finally Colonel Croghan was chosen. Captain Sinclair was placed in command of the small squadron of naval vessels to participate. Then low water and adverse winds delayed them further. It was not until July 12th that they moved into Lake Huron. The brigs *Niagara, Lawrence,* and *Caledonia,* and the schooners *Tigress* and *Scorpion* carried a total of about 700 soldiers.

They intended first to attack a small British post located near the point where the Severn River flows into Georgian Bay. This was the end of one of the main water routes from Lake Simcoe to the Bay and was important for the passage of supplies to Mackinac and the western trading posts. The mouth of the Severn lies at the end of a series of channels among rocks and islands as one approaches it from the open Bay. Even today a local pilot can be helpful to strangers. In 1814 there were no charts or channel markers and the American force was unable to find a pilot. Further, there was a heavy fog. Sinclair groped about in it for several days, doing his best to avoid the rocks. Meanwhile the provisions for the troops he carried were running low. Finally he gave up and sailed away to attack the British post on St. Joseph Island, near Mackinac.

There the Americans discovered that the fort had been abandoned and everything of importance had been removed to Mackinac. They burned what remained, and captured the British schooner *Mink* in the vicinity.

Fort Mackinac was a difficult place to attack. The guns on Sinclair's ships could not be elevated sufficiently to fire on the fort, for it stood some distance above the water. The best landing place seemed to be on the western side of the island, away from the fort—the place where the British had landed when they captured Mackinac. On August 4th Croghan landed there, intending to advance a little distance inland and camp.

McDouall, however, was expecting that landing. Before the Americans had moved half a mile they came under fire from British artillery. The defenders had chosen a position with clear fields of fire to their front and dense woods on either flank. An attempt at a flanking attack met a fierce defence from Indians in the woods. Croghan then tried a frontal attack and suffered a number of casualties. The British forces moved back to still higher ground and the American attack lost momentum completely. Croghan withdrew his force to the protection of the naval guns, with thirteen dead, over fifty wounded, and two captured. McDouall had only a few wounded. He had won a clear victory. The next day an American party with a flag of truce removed the body of Major Holmes, one of their dead, and saw to it that the wounded prisoners were being cared for. Then the Americans sailed away.

Croghan decided once again to look for some of the British installations at the southern end of Georgian Bay. This was in keeping with his original orders, and if he could destroy them it would also serve to cut off the garrison at Mackinac from its base of supply. The *Lawrence, Caledonia,* and *Mink* were sent back to Detroit with all of the militia and two companies of regulars. The *Niagara, Scorpion,* and *Tigress,* carrying three companies of regulars, headed for the mouth of the Nottawasaga, a place considerably easier to find than the mouth of the Severn. Croghan had learned from a prisoner captured on the *Mink* that the British had transferred their supply activities to that point.

In mid-July the British schooner *Nancy* had arrived at the Nottawasaga from Mackinac to pick up supplies. As well as the supplies, a small detachment of seamen were waiting there for her, with Lieutenant Miller Worsley of the Royal Navy. The schooner loaded and set sail for Mackinac; a few hours out she met a boat carrying a message for Worsley from McDouall, saying that American forces were on Lake Huron and directing that the *Nancy* be taken as far up the river as possible and that a blockhouse be built there to protect her. They turned back, and Worsley followed McDouall's instructions. The Nottawasaga River flows parallel to the shore for a number of miles, separated from Georgian Bay only by a long finger of beach and sand dunes, before it breaks through and flows into the Bay. They managed to get the schooner about two miles upstream, but this did not actually remove her from the shore.

On August 13th the American ships arrived. They sent ashore a small party to reconnoitre and soon found the *Nancy* lying in the river behind the long peninsula of sand, next to a blockhouse on the far bank. The following morning the ships moved close to shore and opened fire but with little result because of the sand hills and trees between. The Americans then landed howitzers; these weapons were able to lob shells over the treetops and reach the British position. A shell hit the blockhouse and set it afire. Flames spread to the schooner. She quickly burned and sank. The British party, outnumbered and outgunned, withdrew up the river in two boats and a canoe. The Americans took over the partially burned blockhouse, where they found some official documents and three artillery pieces. They took along the guns and papers, and Croghan and Sinclair sailed off to Detroit in the *Niagara,* while the *Scorpion* and *Tigress,* under command of Lieutenant Daniel Turner, captain of the *Scorpion,* were left on Georgian Bay to prevent British passage between York and Mackinac.

Worsley and his men had been waiting in hiding at a place farther up the river, where they had two *bateaux,* a large canoe, and a quantity of stores. After the American schooners moved away they came down cautiously to the mouth of the Notta-wasaga and proceeded to clear away the trees the Americans had dropped into the channel there. On the night of August 18th they moved quietly into Georgian Bay and started to-wards Mackinac.

Six days later, they unexpectedly came upon the *Scorpion* and *Tigress.* Worsley hid his two *bateaux,* which were large and clumsy, put the body of his men in the big canoe, and slipped by the American vessels at night without being seen, passing within a hundred yards of one of them.

Once at Mackinac, he quickly informed McDouall of de-velopments and obtained his permission to attempt the capture of the two schooners. The small war vessels built on the Lakes by both sides during this time were particularly vulnerable to boat attacks because of their low sides. Sinclair had particular-ly warned Turner of the danger from boarding parties, but the young lieutenant apparently had not been impressed. That night Worsley left Mackinac with four boats, two of which mounted small cannon. With him were his own sailors and a detachment of soldiers from Mackinac under a Lieutenant Bulger. Some Indians in canoes also accompanied them. Wor-sley carefully hid his force during the day and watched for a favourable time to attack. Turner in the *Scorpion* had moved away to cruise off the French River; a canoe brigade from

Montreal, carrying supplies for Mackinac, was hiding a little distance upstream and Turner apparently had gained some knowledge of it. On September 3rd the *Tigress* was alone. That night Worsley struck. At 9:00 P.M. the lookout on the schooner gave warning. The boats closed in on both sides of her and the British forces boarded. After a short, violent battle in which three of the crew were killed and three wounded, the *Tigress* was captured. Sailing-Master Champlin, her captain, had a grape-shot pass through one leg and break the bone of the other. The American prisoners were quickly taken away to Mackinac by boat, and Worsley and most of his men remained on the schooner, mounting their cannon on her in addition to her own.

On the night of September 5th, Turner, in the *Scorpion*, returned to where he had left the *Tigress* and dropped anchor within two miles of her, but exchanged no signals. Worsley slipped his cable at dawn and under only headsails, still flying the American ensign, approached the other schooner. Some of the English officers and men wore the clothing of her former officers and men. The rest of them were concealed, either lying on deck or remaining below. Worsley was only a few yards from Turner's vessel before anyone on her realized that the *Tigress* now had a British crew. The men from the *Tigress* quickly boarded the *Scorpion*. In the brief fight two Americans were killed and two wounded. The total British casualties in both fights were one officer and seven soldiers wounded and three sailors killed.

McDouall praised Worsley highly and recommended him to the naval authorities for promotion. The vessels and stores captured were valued at £16,000. The *Tigress* was renamed *Surprise*, the *Scorpion* was renamed *Confiance*. Once again there was a British naval force on the Upper Lakes.

After these events it was evident that another, larger, American squadron could be expected to return the following year to do the job that this one had failed so miserably to accomplish. The two captured schooners were very nice, but they could easily be overwhelmed by more and bigger vessels sent from Lake Erie. Therefore the British decided to build a really large war ship on Georgian Bay, a frigate of 44 guns. A good harbour that could be defended if necessary was also needed; they had no wish for another *Nancy* episode. Penetanguishene was to be developed into a naval base and the big frigate was to be built there.

The proposed base was surrounded by forest and was thirty miles from Lake Simcoe. A road from Lake Simcoe to Penetanguishene had been discussed in the past; now it was a necessity in order to get supplies to the new base. By the time the decision was made, winter was at hand. A company of the Canadian Fencibles and a body of militia were sent north from York to start building the road. The officer in charge of the project was an army surgeon, Dr. William Dunlop.

In the autumn of 1814 Dr. Dunlop was stationed at York, which he described as "a dirty, straggling village, containing about sixty houses. The church—the only one—was converted into a general hospital, and I formed my lodge in the wing of the Parliament buildings, which had escaped when the Americans had burnt the rest of that fabric." Someone was needed to command the troops that were to build the road. There were no other volunteers. Dunlop took the job and went north to Lake Simcoe.

The troops started at the southern end of the new road and cleared trees steadily towards the north. They worked in snow that sometimes was six feet deep and they had no horses or oxen to help them. Half the men had to pack in the provisions while the other half worked on the road. When the snow became very deep it was necessary to dig a pit around each tree, big enough so that a man could swing his axe. When a log was cut it had to be pulled out of the way by drag ropes. Bridges were built across streams, the men standing waist-deep in the ice-cold water, and ravines were bridged with logs that had to be dragged from the swamps through feet of snow. Members of the expedition lived in shanties made of pine cut in the woods. The primitive buildings only had three walls, for two shanties were always built opposite each other with one fire between. Despite the exposure and heavy work, the health of all concerned was good. The road, such as it was, was pushed through to the harbour.

Towards the end of 1814 Colonel George Head was appointed a commissariat officer to supervise the building of the post at Penetanguishene. He arrived at Halifax from England in November and came to Lake Simcoe in February of 1815. There he overtook a party of a dozen English shipwrights on their way to the new station on Georgian Bay. They all proceeded together, travelling north over the new road. Head rode in a sleigh drawn by a team of horses, probably the first team ever to come to this area. The last ten miles of the road were so bad that they had to unhitch the team and lift the sleigh over fallen trees for two or three hundred yards at a stretch. When they came to the Yeo River (today called the Wye), he followed it to Georgian Bay and then came around the shore to Penetanguishene, travelling on the ice. There he found Captain Collier of the Navy and a mixed group of soldiers and sailors who had preceded him by a few days and who were living in huts similar to those used by Dunlop's crew.

The next evening a gang of Canadian axe-men arrived from York. Early on the morning of March 2nd they began to cut trees and erect log buildings, working, Head noted, with great skill. He busied himself with arranging his own quarters until the 6th of March, when he woke to find the snow covered with a glassy coat of ice and the whole bay nearly frozen over. He went down to the shore and put on a pair of skates; in a few minutes he was moving quickly over the surface.

After he had explored almost every part of Penetanguishene Bay he saw in the distance a strange hump on the ice. Approaching it more closely he saw that it was light brown and noticed that it occasionally moved a little. As he watched it curiously, wondering whether to go and get his gun, the hide was thrown aside and there emerged the head and shoulders of an Indian who had been fishing through the ice. He had wrapped himself in a buffalo skin for warmth. He sat over a hole about a foot square, holding a short spear ready for any fish attracted to his bait of an artificial fish carved from white wood, about 8 or 9 inches long. The Indian was annoyed at the interruption, but his interest was soon aroused by the ice skates Head wore. He also wanted the Englishman's red flannel shirt. Head demonstrated the use of the skates but refused to give up his shirt. "So, shaking him by the hand and patting his shaggy locks, I skated away, leaving him to pursue his occupation for the rest of the evening."

On March 9th Head's new house was completed and he was about to transfer his belongings to it when an Indian messenger unexpectedly appeared and, after some fidgeting, produced an official message from under his shirt. It instructed Head to return to Lake Simcoe and await further orders. The other officers received similar messages, sending them elsewhere. The whole project was to be given up. The treaty of peace had been signed between the United States and England at Ghent in December of 1814 and ratified at Washington on February 17th, 1815. Communications moved slowly, but word finally had reached the frontier station on Georgian Bay.

# Penetanguishene

The British representatives who signed the peace treaty at Ghent were not as effective as their military men had been. They agreed to the mutual restoration of all territory as it was held in 1811. The international boundary westward from Lake Superior was to remain the same; the entire boundary was to be fixed on the ground at a later date by special commissioners. The disgust and disappointment of men like McDouall, who had fought for British interests, were complete. The fur traders reacted even more strongly for they had supported the war with effort and money, expecting that it would insure their continued use of territory to the west. Now the treaty-makers at Ghent had given back to the United States everything that had been won from it. In many ways this was the death-blow for the fur trade, and the merchants knew it. Weakened by the war and treaty, the North West Company was forced in 1821 to combine with the Hudson's Bay Company, and an era came to an end.

Colonel McDouall chose Drummond Island, at the northwestern end of Manitoulin Island, as his new base. The buildings were partly completed when he evacuated Mackinac in July of 1815 and moved his garrison to the new post, and he set about constructing a fort that would be stronger than Mackinac itself, and building a village nearby. The main channel passed to the west of Drummond Island; when the international boundary was surveyed it surely would follow the centre of that channel. Ironically, the boundary survey did not follow the main channel. It gave Drummond Island instead to the United States. And so the British garrison had to move again, this time to Penetanguishene.

Meanwhile, throughout 1815 and 1816 the station at Penetanguishene was maintained by a small caretaker detachment that completed the buildings that had been started, and cleared the shore for a shipyard and docks. Colonel Head, following his orders, busied himself during the summer of 1815 with planning the location of two blockhouses on the Nottawasaga, one at Williow Creek, near the place where the portage reached the river from Lake Simcoe, and one closer to the river mouth. While he was there, boatloads of supplies were moving over Lake Simcoe and passing across the portage and down the river for shipment both to the forts at Mackinac and Drummond Island and to the various North West Company posts. Head went back to Quebec late that summer; the blockhouses were actually erected the next year.

The main fort on the Nottawasaga was built about four miles from the river mouth, at the point where the river comes to the Bay from the hinterland and turns parallel to the shore. Thus it was near the base of the long sand peninsula, difficult to reach but close enough to the shore so that its people could observe anything that approached from the water. Twenty or thirty sailors and marines were stationed there and a few civilians settled nearby. Three small gunboats were built in the spring of 1817.

In 1817 work was begun again at Penetanguishene. A shipwright and a naval artificer were there that summer and the artificer supervised the construction of a powder magazine made of logs. The following summer official vacillation ended; the post on the Nottawasaga was abandoned, largely because of its poor harbour, and the men and vessels there were moved to Penetanguishene, which henceforth would be the only naval station on the Bay. In 1828 Penetanguishene was also made a military post when the garrison was moved from Drummond Island. Both of these developments were too late to be of great strategic importance however. Had a naval or military station been established there after the initial survey of the harbour, made at Governor Simcoe's direction in 1794, or had the various plans been carried out that were discussed before and during the War of 1812, Penetanguishene might have been almost as significant as Mackinac in the history of the Upper Lakes. Instead, it became a backwater, manned by small detachments and harbouring small vessels, and was maintained as a government establishment until 1852 mainly because it guarded the rear approach to the capital of Upper Canada. The memory of the American occupation of York faded slowly.

Though Penetang was not important strategically, it had a unique flavour. For many years it was the only settlement on Georgian Bay; it was a frontier settlement that was so typical it was not really typical at all. Where else could one find such a microcosm of early nineteenth-century Canada? The British element ranged from the private soldier to the upper-middle-class officer; nobility came on occasional visits. A few Britishers acted as traders, merchants, and innkeepers. There were Canadians of pure French descent and many more of mixed French and Indian blood. There were Indians. And there were a few families that had Jewish and Italian strains.

By 1818 some buildings were already standing. That year a hospital, doctor's residence, and guard-house were built. An inn was also constructed of logs by one Thomas Johnstone, a silk mercer, who recently had come from England. Johnstone's wife claimed descent from the Earls of Darnley, and the couple were said to have been married in Westminster Abbey. She cherished a silver teapot given her as a wedding present. Johnstone was a Free Mason of some enthusiasm and therefore named his place the Masonic Arms.

The next year the Duke of Richmond, who was governor-general, and his son-in-law, Sir Peregrine Maitland, the lieutenant-governor, visited Penetanguishene and stayed at the Masonic Arms. Probably as a result of this visit, three local townships that were just being carved out of the wilderness were named Tiny, Tay, and Floss, for the three lap dogs of Lady Sarah Maitland.

In April of 1824 Sir John Franklin, the Arctic explorer, came and stayed for a week at Penetanguishene. His two assistants, Lieutenant Back and Dr. Richmond, were there at least part of the time. Some of the party stayed at the Johnstone establishment, while the *voyageurs* who accompanied them camped on the shore, waiting for additional men and supplies from Montreal. The explorer and his men came on foot over the Nottawasaga portage, and from the River Nottawasaga came around to Penetanguishene by water. Franklin was endeavouring to find a sea passage from the North Atlantic to the North Pacific; on this trip he would go down the Mackenzie River to the Arctic; the North West Passage still lay just over the horizon. At Penetanguishene he wrote his impression of the place to his wife, "I do not think . . . that either you or I would relish such a secluded life. If we could convey our library, it would be the very place for me to get through it." Before the letter was completed, Franklin learned that Lady Franklin had died in London shortly after he had departed, the previous February. Soon after receiving that news he set out in a north-westerly direction, travelling through Lakes Huron and Superior in two large canoes that he had arranged to be waiting for him at Penetang.

When the garrison was moved to Penetanguishene, the great majority of people who had worked for the British forces at Drummond Island migrated with them. Most of these migrants were of French or French-and-Indian descent. They settled at the southern end of Georgian Bay, largely around the establishment at Penetang, and comprised one of the groups of *voyageurs* that settled wherever there were British military or trading posts in Canada. Eventually, for example, the Hudson's Bay Company had canoe brigades stationed as far apart as Montreal, Moose Factory in the Arctic, and Fort Vancouver on the Pacific, and at all of these places there were *voyageurs* to man the canoes. From the earliest days, Frenchmen established, in varying degrees of formality, connections with Indian women. When canoemen or traders found themselves located permanently some distance from Quebec, they often married Indians and settled in those far-away places to raise their families.

The men who came to Penetanguishene were a typical group. They acted as canoemen, boatmen, pilots, guides, hunters, and fishermen. When government officials made the yearly journey to Manitoulin Island to present gifts to the Indians there, they manned the canoes that were used. They also built canoes. One *voyageur* turned blacksmith, Toussant Boucher, made a canoe out of sheet iron. A *canôt du nord* of about twenty-four feet in length, it was paddled by eight or nine men. The iron canoe achieved mild fame; it was used for trips to Manitoulin and on one occasion was part of a fleet that carried a visiting Englishman, Lord Morpeth, on a tour of Lake Huron and delivered him at Detroit. The canoes then coasted the Canadian shore of Lake Erie, were portaged by wagon to Lake Ontario, and finally came to Toronto, where the canoemen were given a rousing welcome. The next year the iron canoe was brought back to Penetanguishene; it was pulled on rollers by teams of horses as far as Lake Simcoe, then followed the water route the rest of the way. Its weight on a portage and its tendency to cut through heavy waves rather than ride over them limited its usefulness. Father Proulx, the priest who commissioned the building of the canoe and who later presented it to the garrison, conceived his idea a hundred years too soon; no metal had yet been developed that was light enough to make a really satisfactory canoe.

The village of Penetanguishene, which was largely French-Canadian, grew up near the inner end of the long, narrow Penetanguishene Bay. The naval and military establishment was somewhat nearer the mouth of the harbour.

Until 1832 only a rude trail covered the two miles from the government establishment to the village; the military road from the south came more directly to the post and did not go through the small settlement. About that year a road was cleared to the village by one A. A. Thompson, who contracted to build both the road and a number of small log houses along it. This was part of a scheme whereby retiring British soldiers were given, instead of a pension, a log house with a small farm behind it and additional land outside the town. They had to enlist for four years as "enrolled pensioners"—reservists of a sort, who could be called upon for light duty, such as standing guard. Halfway along the new road was a reservation for the Church of England, and it was there that the small church of St. James was later built. This settlement became known as the Lines, and through it, the village gained a solid British element. Pensioners brought from England were settled throughout Canada at this time; the group at Penetanguishene, however, appears to have been a little different. The men apparently were intended to be auxiliary to the garrison, and many of them seem to have been recently retired. At least some of them had served in Canada, and a few were stationed at Penetanguishene at the time of retirement. Most of them knew little about farming and some did not even realize that they were losing their pensions by accepting the cottages and grants of land. Few prospered and most who could do so turned soon to other pursuits.

Alfred A. Thompson, builder of the Lines, had arrived in Penetanguishene when he was seventeen years old and had engaged as a clerk with a merchant and fur trader. In time he started on his own, building the first brick store in town. Later he also took over the business of his former employer. Until 1881 he held annual fur sales that were attended by buyers from Montreal, New York, London, Berlin, and even Australia. The Nipissing Indians came annually to Penetanguishene in a fleet of canoes laden with furs, camped on the shore, and spent several days visiting and being visited by traders, before returning home with their yearly supplies. As more settlers came into the surrounding countryside, Thompson's store also became known as the only place in the vicinity where farmers could get cash for their produce in order to pay their taxes. Thompson's younger brother, Henry, later joined in the business. Alfred eventually married the daughter of Quartermaster-Sergeant David Burke, one of the more successful pensioners, and both Thompsons and Burkes may still be found in or near the town.

In 1834 Captain John Moberly was appointed naval commander at Penetanguishene. Moberly was born in Petrograd of English parents, and although he entered the navy when he was twelve years old he apparently maintained his Russian acquaintanceship, for in 1825 he married Mary Fock, daughter of General Fock of the Russian Imperial Army. The Moberlys appear to have been well liked by Canadians, something not always true of recent arrivals from England. Of great interest to the Captain was the establishment of an Anglican church for the naval and military station; he was mainly responsible for the construction of St. James-on-the-Lines.

One of the most sensitive visitors to Penetanguishene during its days as a naval and military station was Mrs. Anna Jameson, an Englishwoman married to a Toronto judge, who made a circuit of the western lakes. She came over Georgian Bay in 1838, travelling with Mr. Jarvis, the chief superintendent of Indian affairs, following the annual ceremony at Manitoulin Island when the Indians were given presents from the government.

There were two canoes, each five-and-twenty feet in length, and four feet in width, tapering to the two extremities, and light, elegant, and bouyant as the sea-mew, when it skims the summer waves: in the first canoe were Mr. Jarvis and myself; the governor's son, a lively boy of fourteen or fifteen, old Solomon the interpreter, and seven voyageurs. My blankets and night-gear being rolled up in a bundle, served for a seat, and I had a pillow at my back; and thus I reclined in the bottom of the canoe, as in a litter, very much at my ease: my companions were almost equally comfortable. I had near me my cloak, umbrella, and parasol, note-books and sketch-books, and a little compact basket always by my side, containing eau de Cologne, and all those necessary luxuries which might be wanted in a moment, for I was well resolved that I would occasion no trouble but what was inevitable. The voyageurs were disposed on low wooden seats, suspended to the ribs of the canoe, except our Indian steersman, Martin, who, in a cotton shirt, arms bared to the shoulder, loose trowsers, a scarlet sash round his waist, richly embroidered with beads, and his long black hair waving, took his place in the stern, with a paddle twice as long as the others.

The party left Manitoulin with the British flag astern, the cheers of the Englishmen, and the yells and gunshots of the Indians saluting them as they went. Their first camp was near the hut of a fur trader and the wigwams of an Indian band that was going home from the recent festivities. Other camps were situated on various rocky islands, where the guest of honour noted, "They pitched my tent at a *respectful* distance from the rest, and made me a delicious elastic bed of some boughs, over which was spread a bear-skin, and over that blankets. . . ." The wild scenery was so magnificent that Mrs. Jameson at times was almost suffocated by her intense appreciation of it. Even bad weather did not dampen the feeling.

> We breakfasted on an island almost covered with flowers, some gorgeous and strange, and unknown, and others sweet and familiar; plenty of the wild pea, for instance, and wild-roses, of which I had many offerings. I made my toilette in a recess among some rocks; but just as I was emerging from my primitive dressing-room, I felt a few drops of rain, and saw too clearly that our good fortune was at an end. We swallowed a hasty breakfast, and had just time to arrange ourselves in the canoe with all the available defenses of cloaks and umbrellas, when the rain came down heavily and hopelessly. But notwithstanding the rain and the dark gray sky, the scenery was even more beautiful than ever.

After two days of stormy weather the travellers came finally to the small post located at the southern end of Georgian Bay. "About nine o'clock we entered the bay of Penetanguishene, so called from a high sand-bank at the entrance, which is continually crumbling away. The expressive Indian name signifies 'Look! it is falling sand!' " Mrs. Jameson was much struck with the natural beauty of the scene, but was less enthusiastic about the post and village.

> We spent the greater part of two days at Penetanguishene, which is truly a most lovely spot. The bay runs up

into the land like some of the Scottish lochs, and the shores are bolder and higher than usual, and as yet all clothed with the primeval forest. During the war there were dockyards and a military and naval depot here, maintained at an immense expense to government; and it is likely, from its position, to rise into a station of great importance; at present, the only remains of all the warlike demonstrations of former times are a sloop sunk and rotting in the bay, and a large stone-building at the entrance, called the "Fort," but merely serving as barracks for a few soldiers from the garrison at Toronto. There are several pretty houses on the beautiful declevity, rising on the north side of the bay, and the families settled here have contrived to assemble round them many of the comforts and elegancies of life. I have reason to remember with pleasure a Russian lady, the wife of an English officer, who made my short sojourn here very agreeable.

There was an inn here, not the worst of Canadian inns; and the *wee* closet called a bed-room, and a little bed with its white cotton curtains appeared to me the *ne plus ultra* of luxury. . . .

At Penetanguishene there is a hamlet, consisting of twenty or thirty log-houses, where a small remnant of the poor commuted pensioners (in all a hundred and twenty-six persons) now reside, receiving daily rations of food, and some little clothing, just sufficient to sustain life.

Among the various regiments stationed at Penetanguishene over the years were several Scottish ones. Their members may have agreed with Mrs. Jameson that the Bay was reminiscent of a loch; they were staunch supporters of the area. One officer wrote, for a St. Andrew's Day banquet at the Masonic Arms, a song which became the anthem of the local Scots for some years afterward.

> *What though removed frae balls and routs*
> *And city's cheerin' gleam*
> *We've got our ain guid salmon trout*
> *At Penetanguishene.*

The naval station was at an especially low ebb during Mrs. Jameson's visit. As the war vessels that had been left after the War of 1812 gradually rotted away and sank, only small craft were maintained. In 1828 Commodore Barrie inspected the establishment and later recommended to the Admiralty that at least one vessel be kept in commission at Penetang. Nothing was done for some time, however. The abortive rebellion at Toronto in 1837 by William Lyon Mackenzie, who fled to the United States and tried to raise an invasion army there, may have led the authorities to think a little more about this back-door approach to the provincial capital. The steamers *Minos, Experiment,* and finally, the *Mohawk* patrolled the Bay in succession until the closing of the base in 1852.

By 1850 settlers were scattered along the southwestern shore of Georgian Bay and small local communities had sprung up where Collingwood and Owen Sound are located today. In the early fifties a railway started north from Toronto and it soon became clear that the line would terminate on Georgian Bay. The military and naval establishment at Penetanguishene had outlived its usefulness; the United States no longer seemed a great threat, and if armed forces were ever needed on Georgian Bay in the future they could be carried there quickly by rail. The *Mohawk* was the last naval vessel at Penetang and a detachment of the Royal Canadian Rifles were the last regular troops. The establishment was closed in 1852 and guarded by the Enrolled Pensioners until 1856. Its facilities were then turned over to the provincial government, which soon converted them into a reformatory.

The frontier had passed beyond Georgian Bay and a new period of development was at hand.

# Red land and white

During the century and a half that passed after the dispersal of the Huron Indians, Algonquin groups drifted into the country and occupied it. When the government of Upper Canada wanted the land near and along the shore of the Bay, the Ojibways, Algonkian people, were living there. In 1798 a treaty was signed for the Indians by five Ojibway chiefs, which, for the sum of £101, ceded to the government a tract of land surrounding Penetanguishene. William Claus, Superintendent of Indian Affairs, signed for the government, and George Cowan signed as interpreter. In 1808 surveys and exploration began in the wilderness area between the Penetanguishene purchase and Lake Simcoe, as the result of a preliminary treaty—an agreement to buy—which had been made with the Indians, but it was not until 1815 that the actual treaty was signed. For this considerably larger piece of land the Indians received £4,000.

Another parcel, all of the remaining land between Lake Ontario and Georgian Bay, totalling 1,592,000 acres, was ceded by the Indians in 1818 in return for an annual payment "forever" of goods to the value of £1,200 in currency. This large area contained among many other things, much of the most fertile and heavily wooded land on the Bay, fronting on the south-western corner of shore, where the towns of Collingwood and Owen Sound later developed. A few small areas within the ceded tract were still reserved for Indian use. In 1836 and 1851 other areas were surrendered in what now is the County of Grey.

Each year at a formal ceremony government officials gave presents to the Indians—such things as cloth, tools, combs, powder and shot, and a few guns and brass kettles for the chiefs. In part this was the annual payment in goods that was specified in the treaties, but as time went on, tribesmen who had no part in the treaties began to attend. Even Indians who lived in United States territory—and who accepted similar gifts from the United States government—appeared at the annual festivities to receive the British gifts. At first the ceremonies were local affairs, such as the ones that took place on Lake Simcoe and were then moved to Present Island, on Georgian Bay, near Penetang, or, those held at Amherstburg, across the river from Detroit. Then in 1836 and 1837 the local ceremonies were consolidated at Manitoulin Island at the northern end of Georgian Bay, to induce the Indians to retreat there voluntarily.

Traditionally the British had cherished the Indians and had been allied with them in wars against the United States to preserve the fur trade and maintain an Indian country free of settlers. The government still considered itself protector of the Indians, yet since the War of 1812 there had been constant pressure to move the Indians out and give the land to others. Thus much thought was given to Indian welfare at exactly the same time much effort was being made to remove the Indians from their holdings; and the two aims combined neatly in a plan to consolidate the tribes on Manitoulin Island.

In 1836 Sir Francis Bond Head became governor. His misgovernment is generally thought to have caused the revolt of December 1837, but his approach to the Indians was thoughtful enough. After visiting some of them on the frontier and seeing how they lived, he was convinced that civilization brought them only squalor, disease, and alcohol. He enthusiastically adopted the plan to remove them from contact with the white men and became its strongest advocate. As a first step, in 1836 he concluded a treaty with the Indians who then claimed ownership of the Saugeen Peninsula (now more often called the Bruce Peninsula since the County of Bruce has embraced it) and moved them to Manitoulin.

In 1837 Mrs. Jameson, on her trip through Lake Huron, visited Manitoulin Island at the time when a general council of tribes was called for a distribution of presents. She had just come from Mackinac, where she had stayed with Henry Schoolcraft, a well known American Indian agent and scholar, and his wife, the grand-daughter of a great chief. Mrs. Jameson and Mrs. Schoolcraft became good friends. The Schoolcrafts introduced her to many Indians, and showed her their homes. Her education was uninfluenced by Canadian politics, and it is interesting that Mrs. Jameson approved of the settlement plan.

> It is objected to this measure that by cutting off the Indians from agricultural pursuits, and throwing them back on their habits of hunting and fishing, it will retard their civilization; that removing them from the reserved land among the whites, their religious instruction will be rendered a matter of difficulty; that the islands, being masses of barren rock, are almost incapable of cultivation; and that they are so far north-west, that it would be difficult to raise even a little Indian corn; and hence the plan of settling the Indians has been termed *unjustifiable*.

> It is true that the smaller islands are rocky and barren; but the Great Manitoolin, Drummond's, and St. Joseph's, are fertile. The soil on which I now tread is rich and good; and all the experiments in cultivation already tried here have proved successful. As far as I can judge, the intentions of the government are benevolent and *justifiable*.

The governor had started towards Georgian Bay for the distribution of presents that year and the council that followed, but he had been overtaken by a messenger telling him that William the Fourth was dead and that young Victoria was on the throne. He turned back to his capital, sending on Mr.

Jarvis, Superintendent of Indian Affairs, to represent him. The Indian ceremonies took place on the shore of Manitowaning Bay, where a few log buildings had been erected to store the gifts and serve the officials. The council met in the large one-room house provided for the superintendent and his officers. "A deal plank, raised on tressels, served as a table; there were a few stools and benches of deal-board, and two raised wooden platforms for beds: such were the furniture and decorations of the grand council-hall in which the *representative* of the representative of their Great Mother had now assembled her red children. . . ." The Indians loved oratory heavily adorned with metaphor and it was standard practice to refer to the king or queen as the Great Father or Great Mother of the red men and to them as the children.

> The council met about noon. At the upper end of the log-house I have mentioned, stood the chief superintendent, with his secretary or grand vizier, Major Anderson; the two interpreters, and some other officials . . . near me I perceived three Methodist missionaries and two Catholic priests. The chiefs came in, one after another, without any order of precedence. . . .

The superintendent addressed the group, saying, "Children, —when your Great Father, the lieutenant governor, parted with his Red children last year at this place, he promised again to meet them at the council-fire, and witness in person the grand delivery of presents now just finished." Jarvis then explained that their Great Father had been called back to Toronto because of the death of their Great Father on the other side of the Great Salt Lake and the accession of Queen Victoria. He went on to say that the British could not continue indefinitely to give presents to Indians living in the United States, but that those tribes would be welcome to move to Manitoulin. He urged the Indians to listen to the clergymen living among them when they spoke on the subject of religion but to remember that they had nothing to do with temporal affairs (evidence of normal friction between missionaries and civil authorities). He presented them with a flag, and entreated them to abstain from the use of firewater.

In the speeches that followed, one chief asked that the meetings be held in the future on the St. Mary's River and objected to residing on Manitoulin; the others who spoke, however, agreed to Manitoulin as a place for their tribes to live. After some further ceremony and a small distribution of extra presents to important Indians, it all came to an end. Mrs. Jameson remarked, "The council then broke up, and I made my way into the open air as quickly as I could."

When Mrs. Jameson left Georgian Bay later, after visiting Penetanguishene, she departed from the little settlement of Coldwater, near the southeastern end of the Bay. The chief Yellowhead and some of his people whose lands were in that area had recently petitioned for legal titles. The irony of this was not lost on her and she exclaimed, ". . . and they *humbly* entreat (these original lords of the soil!) as a particular boon, that their 'little bits of land' may be secured to their children and posterity for ever."

The plans for an Indian settlement on Manitoulin were grander than anything that ever developed, but the island did become the centre of activity for the Indian department, and Captain Anderson (Mrs. Jameson seems to have promoted him when she called him major) was moved in 1838 from the Indian reservation at Coldwater to Manitowaning on the island. He made the trip in October, accompanied by thirty-three other people in an open *bateau*. In addition to his own wife and four children, there were a missionary and his family, a schoolmaster and his family, a doctor and his family, plus servants and workmen. There were also a cat and a dog, and in addition the *bateau* was laden with all the belongings and provisions it could carry.

The voyage lasted twenty-one days. The open craft provided no protection against rain, snow, or freezing spray. The camp they made on the shore each afternoon consisted of two tents and one wigwam; there were no other shelters. The party only travelled for a few hours each day because it took so long to organize the camp for the families. Each morning before they started again the ice had to be cut away to free the *bateau*.

Finally they approached their destination, Manitowaning. The travellers could see three log buildings in which they were to live, but one of them was in flames. By the time they had landed nothing remained but ashes. That night the party moved into what was supposedly Captain Anderson's own small house. The four families divided up the rooms; the single men slept on the kitchen floor. Other workmen, who were already on the scene and whose carelessness had caused the fire, occupied the other log building.

The four families and their servants, a total of twenty-eight people, remained under Captain Anderson's roof. The day after their arrival one of Anderson's daughters heard a loud sobbing in the room below. She peeped through a knothole in the floor and saw the body of the schoolmaster's infant son lying on a table; he had died from exposure on the trip. Six weeks later the doctor's child died. A schooner, which was to bring supplies, was unable to get through the ice and had to turn back to Penetanguishene. It was not until the next spring that another *bateau* arrived, its crew half expecting to find everyone dead.

The remainder of them had survived, however, eating potatoes, maple sugar, game, and fish. Soon building operations began and before long each family had their own home. Log houses were built for workmen and Indians, a workshop for carpenters and coopers, and a blacksmith shop. The village of Manitowaning sprang to life.

By 1854 other tribes had moved into the Saugeen Peninsula, which had been vacated by Head's treaty almost twenty years earlier. White settlement was pushing close, and so another treaty was concluded with the later occupants, and the peninsula was ceded again. Again certain reservations were kept for the use of the Indians, but much of this reserved land was also ceded in later treaties. Land ownership for the Algonquins, who were a semi-nomadic people, was less formal and permanent than it was to the white race, and was based more on immediate possession than on legal title. This was, in part, why they gave up their lands with so little resistance.

The acquisition of Indian land by white men, throughout a long and chequered history, has too frequently been accompanied by too little recompense and too much moral sanction. The treaty of 1854 ended with the sentence, "And we hereby request the sanction of our Great Father the Governor General to the surrender which we consider highly conducive to our general interests." It was signed by a number of Indian chiefs, but one suspects that a white man had something to do with the writing.

In addition to the groups who settled on Manitoulin, other tribal fragments were moved to other reservations, such as the one on Christian Island at the southern end of Georgian Bay. Some Indians doubtless retreated farther west as the whites advanced; some were absorbed into white communities. A few minor treaties were signed in order to tidy up what small pieces of land remained. By the end of the nineteenth century most of the arable land around Georgian Bay was taken by people of European descent.

Soon after the treaties were signed the surveyors appeared on the land. The first of these was Samuel S. Wilmot who pioneered exploration of the area around Penetanguishene in 1808, established the first line for the Penetanguishene Road in 1811, and laid out town sites at either end of it in 1812. He also laid out lots for settlement along the road. Other surveyors followed. An officer of the Royal Engineers did some of the early work establishing the lines of the townships near Penetang. Generally, however, civilian surveyors were retained. They were often paid, either in part or in full, by grants of land in the areas they surveyed. They were first on the ground and had the opportunity to select the best. Therefore any settler who had to buy land usually tried to buy surveyors' script, or title, rather than take up a grant.

A land surveyor was both engineer and explorer. He went through country that few if any white men had seen before. He established the lines for roads and subdivided the countryside into packages that could be granted to settlers and others. He picked the locations for towns and laid out the town sites. It was a demanding job and the surveyors were either very good or very bad. Many of the careless or incompetent surveys have been redone over the intervening years, but some remain to this day to plague landowners.

After the surveyors, came the settlers. The first settlers on Georgian Bay took up land near the naval base at Pene- tanguishene in 1818 and the years immediately following. They were the civilians who provided goods and services to the men at the establishment; the earliest kept taverns. By 1820 farming settlers had taken up land at either end of the Penetanguishene Road, both where it began at Lake Simcoe and within a few miles of where it ended, at Penetang. About 1828, when the garrison at Drummond Island was transferred to Penetanguishene, there was an influx of *voyageurs* and others who depended upon the armed forces and the trading companies, and who settled near the new military post.

In 1835 a group of investors set out to colonize St. Joseph Island, near Sault Ste. Marie. A military post had been es- tablished on the island in 1796, and though it had afterward been abandoned, the title still remained with the government. Thus there was no question of Indian ownership and the government was willing to sell the land for a shilling per acre.

The moving spirit behind the colony was Major William Kingdom Rains, a retired British army officer then living on the south shore of Lake Simcoe. One of his partners owned the new Georgian Bay steamer *Penetanguishene*, and it was part of the plan that she would be the supply vessel for the enter- prise, operating between Coldwater, at the head of a portage from Lake Simcoe, and St. Joseph Island. That May the partners steamed out of Penetang Bay in the little vessel with a cargo of building materials and a passenger list of workmen. On the afternoon of the third day they arrived at a beautiful inlet on the island, and soon afterwards they set ashore the men, who went to work clearing land and building shelters. The steamer made another trip and returned with some mill- wrights and a few settlers. The workmen had previously found a stream ideally situated for a mill, which now rose quickly, together with a store.

The settlement project failed, however, partly because Rains lost most of his money as the result of speculation by his agent in London. There was then no capital with which to bring in and establish settlers. By 1839 the settlement had only ten

55

houses, eight of which were inhabited by French Canadians and half-breeds who probably were there when the Major arrived. Rains lived on a farm some ten miles west of the village. He withdrew from the settlement company which, however, continued to do some business in shipping fish and maple sugar by schooner to Detroit and Chicago.

Rains himself was by far the most interesting part of the whole venture. He had travelled widely in Europe, spoke several languages, and brought with him to St. Joseph Island an extensive library. He also brought with him two attractive sisters, Frances and Eliza Doubleday, well-educated daughters of an English attorney. Major Rains had been legally separated from his wife some years before and had established his relationship with Frances Doubleday soon afterwards; when they came to Canada they brought their first child with them. At first Eliza seems to have lived with them as any young spinster might live in the household of a married sister. But after they had resided for a time on St. Joseph Island, where the Major was the only man of education or background, the situation changed. The two sisters were devoted to each other, but they also found that they were both in love with the same man.

The trio arrived at a solution that could only have worked in such a remote spot. Rains set up two houses, side by side, one for each of the women. He gave his name to the children of each, and the two families grew up together in harmony and affection. From the viewpoint of those concerned it seems to have been a good arrangement. The two mothers were well qualified to teach their children, and both families had books from the library to study.

Those not directly concerned with the arrangement were apt to register indignation when they heard the story. William Cullen Bryant, who passed by on a ship but did not stop, commented, "The English polygamist has been more successful in seeking solitude than in avoiding notoriety." But Louis Agassiz and a companion who landed at St. Joseph Island in 1848 discovered that the Major was quite an interesting person:

As we landed, a rather rough-looking, unshaven personage in shirt-sleeves walked up and invited us to his house, which was close at hand. We found his walls lined with books; Shakespeare, Scott, Hemans, etc., caught my eye as I passed near the shelves, forming a puzzling contrast with the rude appearance of the dwelling. A very few moments sufficed to show a similar contrast in our host himself. He knew Professor Agassiz by reputation, had read reports of his lectures in the newspapers, and evinced a warm interest in the objects of our excursion. . . . His conversation, eager and discursive, running over Politics, Science and Literature, was that of an intelligent and well-read man. . . . He turned out to be an ex-Major in the British Army, and he showed us a portrait of himself in full regimentals, remarking with a smile that he had once been noted as the best-dressed man in his regiment.

The heavy forests on the southwesterly shore of the Bay—the fertile area between the Nottawasaga River and the southern end of the Bruce Peninsula—were surveyed in the 1830's and 1840's. Charles Rankin, one of the ablest practitioners, did much of the work along this shore. Rankin, an energetic man with a firm jaw, first started out in 1833, travelling by boat from Penetang, where he hired a number of men to assist him, and going off into the wilderness despite warnings of fierce animals and savage Indians. At least one settler had already preceded him; about 1825 John A. Vail had established himself at what still is called Vail's Point, in St. Vincent Township, at the outer end of Owen's Sound.

In 1833 Rankin built a log house for himself near the present town of Thornbury, clearing a field a little distance to the west of the house and planting potatoes. The same year an Irishman named Richard McGuire took up land nearby. Rankin was not truly a settler, for he moved on when his surveys on Georgian Bay were completed; McGuire, however, brought his family and settled permanently.

In 1840 Rankin arrived at the mouth of the Sydenham River—the site of the city of Owen Sound—to lay out a town. Tangled evergreens covered the little valley and leaned across the stream, meeting overhead. The river was choked with fallen trees and its marshy banks swarmed with mosquitoes. Rankin first began his survey in the part of the valley where the Indians were living, but when they expressed strong indignation he discreetly moved over to the other side and there laid out the new town.

In October of that year several men landed in a sailboat at the Indian village and were directed to the surveyor's camp. They went on up the river, struggling through the trees fallen across it and chopping them away where necessary, until they reached the wigwam Rankin had erected for himself. He was nowhere to be seen, but a horn lay on a stump nearby. One of the newcomers, John Telfer, picked up the horn and blew it, and presently the surveyor emerged from the woods.

Telfer was a land agent. He was a competent Scot who already had experience in bringing out his countrymen to settle elsewhere in Upper Canada, and for this reason he had been appointed by the government to open up the land surrounding the inlet called Owen's Sound, to locate settlers there, to build roads, and to build houses and a church for the Indians. Because it was late in the year, Telfer had time only to see to the construction of the log building that was to be his headquarters and to work with Rankin in laying out part of the valley in small lots. On the 11th of November he left the scene and did not return until the next spring. One of the men who had accompanied him remained, however, and lived in the log building all winter. He was Thomas Rutherford, a second cousin of Sir Walter Scott, and he became the first permanent resident of that area. The following spring Telfer returned, bringing with him his sixteen-year-old daughter, Elizabeth. During the spring and summer roads were cut, Indian houses were built, and the settlers who began to arrive were given their locations. The settlement was called Sydenham Village.

Parcels of land in Upper Canada during the first half of the nineteenth century were handed out freely to many people who never settled on them. Descendants of United Empire Loyalists, retired military and naval men, and others due rewards for public service, were given sizeable grants. Much of this land was held for resale, sometimes for many years, and

58

was not occupied. As a result, large tracts of land that had been granted remained unsettled and wild. Charles Rankin was asked for information on the situation in 1838, when Lord Durham was gathering evidence for his report on the causes of the uprisings of the previous year, and said that at that time all of the land in the townships of Nottawasaga and Collingwood, at the southernmost end of Georgian Bay, had been granted, but that they were almost entirely unoccupied, the Township of Collingwood having only one settler.

Not only did the absentee landowners block settlement, but they refused to pay taxes. Thus great areas provided no funds to build the roads and schools necessary to support immigrants. No one would build that practical necessity, a grist mill, in such an area. Local governing bodies struggled with this problem for years. When they tried to sell the land for unpaid taxes the grantees came into court with the plea that technically the land still belonged to the Crown; they merely had sole licence to use it whenever they decided to do so.

Although land was granted freely to absentees who had the slightest claim on the government, it was often difficult for a legitimate settler to get land at all. A description of what the settler had to go through has been given by the Reverend Thomas Williams, a Methodist clergyman who as a boy came to the area just south of Georgian Bay when his father settled there in 1822, and who for a time in his youth acted as a land agent's helper in establishing settlers.

In my boyhood I have listened to many sad tales by the old settlers of their difficulties in getting their land, the weariness and humiliation of their attendance upon the officers connected with the location of homes in the unclaimed domain of the province. First, there was to be a petition to the Governor-in-Council, presenting the applicant's claim, his antecedents, his present purposes, etc., etc. This would go before the Executive Council, which was presided over by the Governor, and its members were the magnates of the land—clerical, military, and civil—and it was supposed to meet once a week.

59

This it might do or it might not, as the whim or convenience of some of its leading members would determine. The petitioner must then wait, spend time and money, or go away and come again; this is if his means, patience, and loyalty did not wear away in the meantime. If the prayer of the petition was granted, a document was given which he must carry to the office of the Honourable Commissioner of Crown Lands, from thence to the Surveyor-General's office, until a location ticket was obtained.

Upper Canada was a frontier province governed by an aristocratic clique; a home-grown aristocracy made up largely of professional men and merchants, but an aristocracy none the less. The courtesy which prospective settlers received from officialdom depended somewhat upon their station. Retired army and navy officers, for example, usually found that their way was eased in every reasonable manner. Members of the more lowly classes—who were probably much better farmers —not only had to suffer official disinterest, but had also to deal with government clerks who considered themselves superior to the applicants, and yet were not above soliciting petty bribes for attending to government work.

Three main settlement arteries led to Georgian Bay in the first half of the nineteenth century, all of them from Lake Simcoe. The newest was the Coldwater Road and for a time after the inauguration of steamer travel on Lake Simcoe in 1832 it became the most important. Travellers came from York to the foot of the Lake, thence by steamer to its head, and finally by wagon or foot to Coldwater, where they could take small craft down the Coldwater River to the Bay. In 1837 Mrs. Jameson crossed it in the other direction and pronounced it "most detestable." In 1844 the wagon road was extended from Coldwater to Sturgeon Bay, the southeasterly tip of Georgian Bay. It is a measure of the importance placed by the government on the settlers' use of this road that the land agent John Telfer had as one of his duties in the early 1840's the development of the Coldwater Road.

By the 1850's the road, originally cleared to a width of sixty feet or more, was so hemmed in by second growth that passengers were nearly hooked out of the stages by branches as they passed. The newer stretch was so bad that it was almost no road at all; rather it gave the impression of a rough stream bed; the shaking they received in passing over it impressed travellers mightily. At Coldwater, where the two lengths of road joined, there was a sort of tavern, a large frame building meant originally as a school for Indians, but the Indians had long since gone. An English traveller, William H. G. Kingston, arriving there late one night in 1853, reported, "We found, on entering the house, a large hall, which served as bar-room, kitchen, sitting-room, and sleeping-room for the family, where a half-awake woman in a nightcap was serving out drams to a number of rough-looking men." Despite its rigours, this was the most frequently travelled route at the time. Its northern end was the starting point for the pioneer steamers on Georgian Bay.

The Penetanguishene Road, leading from the present site of Barrie, on Lake Simcoe, north to the garrison town on Georgian Bay, was used by troops marching to and from that station, by drovers bringing cattle to the military and naval establishment, and by visitors to the establishment and the town. The first Georgian Bay settlers travelled this way. It was considerably longer than the Coldwater Road, however, and probably for that reason it was not much used by settlers going elsewhere on the Bay than to Penetang.

The Nine-Mile Portage, the tortuous and overgrown Willow Creek, and the Nottawasaga River made up the third, and oldest, route. Travellers came overland from Lake Simcoe, sometimes with the help of oxen or horses to pull their belongings, travelled down the creek and river, and continued their journeys across Georgian Bay.

In 1833 a crude wagon road was cut following the portage, and then roughly parallelled the Nottawasaga River to the shore of Georgian Bay. From there wagons could go for miles along the hard-packed sand, either to the west, towards the newer lands, or to the northeast, towards the areas settled earlier.

Though the road was very bad, after it was built the River became less important as a highway.

In the 1830's settlement began inland along the Nottawasaga River. The mouth and the lower part of the River provided a harbour for small vessels. As settlement spread to the hinterland, use of the harbour continued, but it was a tricky haven. A sand bar across the mouth of the River restricted deep vessels from the harbour. Once in, a sailing vessel might have to wait some time to get out, for the prevailing north and north-west winds blow directly into the river mouth. A strong north-wester would make the water off the harbour untenable; wind and waves swept unhindered the length of Georgian Bay and broke against the shore with full strength.

There was talk of a railway from Toronto to Georgian Bay during the 1830's. At that time a company was formed to build such a line, and in 1837 its backers approved their engineer's recommendation that its terminus be at the mouth of the Nottawasaga. That was a year of panic and depression, however, and the Rebellion followed. The necessary money could not be raised. The scheme was postponed and then practically abandoned until 1844, when it was revived. Construction began at Toronto in 1851 on the first stretch of the road, which was to go to Barrie. In 1852 five separate routes were surveyed from Barrie to various points on Georgian Bay; two of the five led to the Nottawasaga mouth. It was generally assumed by those who owned land there that the Nottawasaga would be chosen as the terminus; the town of Hythe had been laid out at the river mouth and only awaited development of the port to give it life.

Then in 1852 the big two-masted schooner *H. B. Bishop* of Buffalo came to the Nottawasaga to load grain from the farms along the shore and up the River. She was a centreboard vessel drawing only four feet when her board was raised—and when she was empty. She could then enter the mouth of the river when the wind permitted, but if she were afterwards loaded with grain she would draw too much to get out again. The *H. B. Bishop* therefore anchored off shore and waited while the grain was lightered out in boats and scows, a common practice on the Lakes wherever there was no harbour. Before much grain was loaded a storm broke out of the north-west and beat against the schooner, which still was light and riding high. Her anchors dragged on the sandy bottom; she came in sideways and rode so far up on the beach that her crew were able to step ashore; and she ended a total loss. Thus the deficiencies of the harbour were neatly spotlighted at a crucial time.

Ten miles west of the Nottawasaga mouth was Hen and Chickens Harbour, so called from the one large and several lesser islands that gave shelter to what was essentially an open roadstead. A little settlement clung to the shore there. Not long after the *Bishop* wreck the Northern Railway announced that its Georgian Bay terminus would be at Hen and Chickens. The town of Hythe was never built. The first train came to Georgian Bay in 1855, drawn by a funnel-stacked, wood-burning loco-motive, arriving at what had been Hen and Chickens but was now renamed Collingwood.

# The bay develops

As the nineteenth century passed its mid-point, Champlain might still have recognized the shores of Georgian Bay. Most of them were covered by thick forest. The future was plain to see, however, in the many little clearings between Penetanguishene and the new, bustling town of Sydenham.

Life in most of those clearings was primitive. When a settler first arrived, his most pressing concern was usually to build a shanty, a tiny one-room building that would give him (and his family if they were with him) shelter while he cleared some land. Normally the shanty was constructed of small logs, with a roof of elm bark or basswood troughs—split basswood logs with the centres hollowed out. Often there were no windows. The floor was usually of earth, sometimes with a level stump left in the middle for a table. Other furniture was made on the spot with axe and knife. If the shanty was built in the spring there might be no chimney, only a hole in the roof; as winter approached, a fireplace and chimney would be constructed from stone or from clay and sticks. The fireplace served both for cooking and for heating.

Such buildings naturally were shared with the local wildlife, but not often to the extent described by one early settler in the County of Grey:

> So innumerable were the swarms of wood mice (sometimes known as deer mice) that we found it impossible to

keep our food or wheat in any place where they could not get at them, except the round iron bake-kettle with close-fitting lid. Close [sic] wooden boxes were of no use. Their numbers seemed to increase ten-fold and so great did the plague become that it became a problem whether they would drive us out and take possession. So daring were they that if we left the table a moment to fetch the tea or coffee pot they would snatch our ham and bread from our plate and run away with it. My brother often caught them with his hands and killed them as he sat at the table. Their numbers increased as the fall and winter came on. At night we would often be awakened by mice pulling our hair and cutting the bed covers in order to get the cotton wadding or our hair to make themselves nests.

The wooden shanty was only a temporary structure, designed to last until the settler constructed a log house. This usually had to wait upon the arrival of other families in the neighbourhood, for a larger building required the labour of several men. If he had a number of boys, or if he had a little money and was able to hire labour, a pioneer might erect a good log cabin to begin with. Those moving into an established community might board with someone else until they could build their own houses. The majority began with a shanty, however, and a luckless few never attained the opulence of a log cabin.

The first crops were potatoes, turnips, peas, and wheat or oats sown among the stumps. If he prospered, or if he started with some money in pocket, a man soon had domestic animals as well. Oxen were the most useful, for they gave help in clearing land. Few pioneers used horses; they came later, when more land had been cleared. Sheep and pigs usually did not appear until a structure could be built to protect them from the wolves and bears that ranged the forest. Wolves sometimes attacked even such large animals as cows, and bears smashed into sheds to kill pigs and carry them away.

When the settler could spare time from the constant work of clearing ground, he might catch some fish, or if he owned a gun he might shoot a deer or some rabbits. The great flocks of passenger pigeons were also a source of food, but they had the fiendish habit of descending in hordes on newly planted fields and gobbling up all of the precious seed.

Chief Justice Latchford gave a vivid description of the aesthetic splendour of the birds in a field:

> I once saw a large flock feeding in a pea field between me and the sun, low, but bright. The splendid iridescence of their plumage thus received a new glory. Every bird was moving, those left in the rear where the gleaning had been gathered flying over those in front in a constant progression. The vivid colours, flashing wings and rapid and graceful motion combined to produce a scene that is vivid in my memory to-day, after a lapse of more than fifty years.

C. A. Fleming, who had been a resident of the County of Grey as a boy in the 60's, recalled that the pigeons were just as voracious after the crops had matured:

> When the wheat was ripe in early August and cut and stooked, it was quite interesting to see a flock of a few thousand pigeons circle the field and alight on the stooks of wheat. They would entirely cover the grain heads where they were exposed.

The settlers, for their part, were ruthless in their massacre of the birds. This wholesale slaughter, combined with disease, the destruction of the forests, and other factors reduced the flocks. By 1885 the birds were scarce. In 1902 the last of the passenger pigeons recorded on Georgian Bay were seen at Penetanguishene.

Most settlers had no money to hire labourers. When anyone had a large job to be done, his neighbours gathered to help him with it; they held a bee. When land was first being cleared, logging bees were common. Men came together to clear underbrush, cut down trees, and make piles for burning. A grog boss was appointed for every two or three piles, to carry around a pail of whiskey and a dipper. House-raising bees and barn-raisings were also frequent in the early days of settlement, and of course the new buildings were christened with a suitable amount of spirit. Bees and barn-raisings usually grew into prolonged celebrations that offered some relief from grim backwoods reality.

The pioneer housewife tended the interior of the home, cooked the food over the open fire, and made the soap. She and her daughters also made the family's clothing. Most women could spin yarn; those who could weave cloth and owned a loom usually did work for their neighbours as well as for themselves. After the cloth was made it was dyed, again by the women. Pioneer women frequently did a part of the outdoor work as well. Some of them handled a flail or an axe as effectively as a man.

The Queen's Bush, as the Crown lands southwest of the Bay were called, drew people of many backgrounds. Most numerous of all nationalities were the Scots, who emigrated from both highlands and lowlands to settle in Canada. There were many Irish. Germans gathered around the town of Neustadt. English settlers were scattered throughout the area, as were some from the United States. There also were groups of Negroes, made up of slaves who had escaped from the States.

The most successful of the settlers, at least initially, were those of Canadian background who came from other settlements established a generation earlier, for they knew how to meet the problems of frontier life. Some of them even returned to their old homes during the winter, to work there and make money to improve their holdings. This could be a risky move, however; more than one man who went back to his old settlement the first winter returned in spring to find that someone else had taken over his shanty and would not move out.

The isolation and poverty of many of the early settlers were extreme. Flora McAlmon, a well-liked woman who lived in the settlement called the Scotch Line, now the village of Duntroon about five miles south of present-day Collingwood, died in childbirth. Neither doctor nor midwife was to be had. Only one family in the settlement was able to provide lumber to build a coffin; they just had cut down some pine trees and had laboriously sawn them by hand into boards. That family also had a hammer and nails, both comparative rarities in Scotch

Line, and so one of its members worked most of that night to build the coffin.

The English traveller William H. G. Kingston visited Collingwood by steamer in 1853, two years before the town burst into active life upon the arrival of the Northern Railway.

> On looking out, I saw a range of wood-covered hills, a saw-mill, and several plank-houses, the principal one a large store which had suddenly arisen on the forest-shore. To the left we could distinguish the long cutting through the forest, made for the railway, which already reaches close down to the water; and to the right were the rocks, called the Hen and Chickens, said to constitute it a safe harbour.

The railway dock was not completed, so the steamer anchored in the harbour and those going ashore went in by boat. It was not yet much of a town. Everywhere the ground was covered with wood in some form; either the logs, branches, and chips cut from the forest being cleared away, or else the timbers and lumber that were going into new buildings. Most of the streets were still filled with stumps three or four feet high; others were mere lines of blazes on forest trees not yet cut.

When the Northern Railway reached Collingwood in 1855, the town grew quickly. John Disturnell, writing one of his travel guides two years later, gave quite a different description:

> Great numbers of travelers and emigrants are at this point transferred to magnificent steamers, bound for Mackinac, Green Bay, Chicago, and the Great West, as well as to the Saut [*sic*] Ste Marie and Lake Superior. Here are a long pier, 800 feet in length; a breakwater, and light-house; several large stores and storehouses; four hotels, and two or three churches in the course of erection.

According to Disturnell, the town had about 2,000 inhabitants in 1857.

The influence of the railway was felt well beyond Collingwood. Frequent steamer service to Owen Sound—formerly the village of Sydenham—extended that influence along the south-western shore. Manufactured goods were more readily imported and became more plentiful. Settlement increased and the building of rural roads into the towns was stimulated. Farmers had a better market for wheat and other crops that could be shipped by rail. Above all, stands of timber now had some value and the small lumber mills along that shore had a way to send their products to the outside world; the first expansion began in what had been mainly a local Georgian Bay lumber industry.

The Bruce Peninsula was opened for settlement and its lands were first sold in September of 1856. The sales coincided with a land boom, but the bubble exploded the following year. Lands in the Bruce were also burdened with a scheme intended to bring more money into the coffers of the Indian nations who had ceded the peninsula. Timber rights were sold apart from the land itself, and the settlers, until after they had paid the full price of their holdings, were only permitted to cut down those trees necessary to erect their farm buildings.

At that time almost all pioneers bought their land under a plan that allowed them to pay for it over a period of several years. Settlers on the Bruce, however, found themselves in an almost impossible predicament. Mortgages, based on greatly inflated values that had now evaporated, were held on most of their lands. Their debts could only be paid through the productivity of the land itself, yet the settlers were neither permitted to sell the trees produced by their land nor to clear them away and till the soil. When the lumbermen got around to cutting down the trees, it became apparent that the soil was in many places far more rocky and far less fertile than in the lands a short distance to the south. We may imagine the anger with which settlers watched the lumbermen take their trees, and the despair with which they discovered that the forests had grown on limestone or gravel that could not be cultivated.

Settlers began to abandon their holdings in the Bruce, and would-be settlers, who now could see the trap, refused to move in. In 1866 parts of Manitoulin Island were opened for settlement, and this further diminished the appeal of the Bruce Peninsula. A number of minor adjustments were made by the government, in attempts to ease the problem, but it was not until 1882 that the government came effectively to the rescue of settlers on the peninsula and refused to permit the lumbermen to continue taking the trees at will.

As the settlements at the southern end of Georgian Bay matured, attention turned towards the North Shore, which as yet was undeveloped. In 1863 William Beatty, of Thorold, with two of his sons and his son-in-law, sailed along the North Shore in a small boat, looking for timber limits that they might buy. Legend says that they took shelter from a storm in the body of water then called Parry's Sound, midway up that shore; in any event, they learned that a small mill near the mouth of the Seguin River, and some of the adjoining timber limits, were for sale. Shortly afterward they bought the package, called the "Parry Sound Estate," from W. M. and J. A. Gibson.

The younger William Beatty, second son of the elder, was then twenty-eight years old. He had received his M.A. degree in 1863 from Victoria University, and was given the LL.B. in 1864. In 1863 he was also a candidate for the Assembly of Upper Canada on the Reform ticket. Nonetheless he became so enamoured of the Parry Sound area that he decided to become resident manager of the family interests there. For the rest of his life Beatty was the moving spirit of the town of Parry Sound.

Young William Beatty became the very model, in small scale, of the paternalistic tycoon of the nineteenth century. He was a member of the Reform party, and like many reformers in all periods felt that he knew what was best for society, even though society might happen to disagree. He was also a Wesleyan Methodist, and thus was a member of a strongly evangelistic body. This side of William's character became well known around Georgian Bay after 1867, when the Beattys purchased the townsite of Parry Sound and laid out the town. Any person who bought land within the site was required to sign an agreement that no liquor would be sold or traded on the property. The Beatty Covenant, as the agreement was called, was legally valid; after all, Beatty was both a lawyer and a clever man; and it was not until 1950 that the restriction was dissolved by a special act of the Legislature. The effect of this local prohibition was somewhat diluted when the village of Parry Harbour sprang up nearby in the early 70's. There liquor was sold freely in hotels and a store, and there loggers in from the bush could find the relaxation they craved.

Needless to say, William Beatty also saw to the religious life of his townspeople. According to the Missionary Report of the Wesleyan Methodist Church for 1869:

> Five years ago Parry Sound was known only as the hunting ground of the Indians; it is now a thriving village in the very heart of the Free Grant Districts. Immediately after the selection of this plan by the Messrs. J. and W. Beatty (worthy Wesleyans) for the location of their large lumbering establishments, a tide of immigration at once set in. For the accommodation of their workmen and the incoming settlers . . . Mr. William Beatty, the resident partner, erected forthwith at his own expense a neat and commodious Wesleyan Church, deeded it to the Conference, free and unencumbered, and for four years with the assistance of one or two other brethren he has conducted a public religious service twice every Sabbath, led a class meeting at the close of the morning service, and superintended a flourishing Sabbath School in the afternoon.

It is unlikely that anyone who disagreed violently with Beatty settled in his town. Those who did settle there found that he took good care of them. The Beatty firm planted shade trees, saw to it that a road was opened to Bracebridge, in the Muskoka district, thus providing a way into the town by land, and ran the first stages over the road. It also built the steamer *Waubuno* near Thorold in 1856. (She was then towed to Collingwood where her machinery was installed, and she was put in service between that port and Parry Sound.) The Beatty firm's headquarters were in what nominally was their store, and at a time and place that real money was uncommon they made trade easier by circulating their own money, Beatty Script, known locally as "Waubuno Notes."

In 1872 William Beatty Junior bought out the interests of his father and brother in the Parry Sound operation. The next year he married Isabella Bowes, the daughter of the President of the Toronto and Guelph Railway. She was as ardent a Wesleyan as he, and became organist in the Methodist Church at Parry Sound, a post that she filled for the next twenty years. About this time Beatty acquired the honorary title of "Governor" from the townspeople; he was so called locally for the remainder of his life.

A new land-settlement system of free grants had come into being in 1868. The Ontario government, which assumed control of land settlement in 1867, upon Confederation of Canada, could benefit from the mistakes of all previous systems. A new wave of settlers flowed into the Georgian Bay area, though not in the great numbers attracted earlier by the lands in the southwestern corner of the Bay. They must soon have found that much of the land was not fertile and that the rock of the Canadian Shield lay under the forests of the district; the sad remains of abandoned farms suggest the heartbreak of their former owners. Perhaps some of them were lucky and found employment in Parry Sound, where Beatty and others were building additional mills and factories. But it is not surprising that in 1892 a sizeable group of people from the Parry Sound district migrated to the Edmonton area, then in the North-West Territories, or that another 200 families went in 1894. Neither is it surprising that the migrants found their old farms had little market value when they left them.

The only lumber centre on the North Shore, other than Parry Sound, to achieve any permanence was Byng Inlet, at the mouth of the Magnetawan River. The town was named for the body of water on which it stood, which in turn was named for Admiral John Byng. In 1871 two lumber companies had mills at the town, and by 1890 there were three of them. In that year the mills of Byng Inlet cut more lumber than those at any other point on Georgian Bay.

Local marine traffic continued to grow and to tie the Georgian Bay communities together. The people of Owen Sound and Byng Inlet, for example, knew far more about each other in the 70's and 80's than they do today. In 1876 the steamer *Northern Belle* was placed in local service connecting the towns of Collingwood and Owen Sound, the North Shore ports, and Sault Ste. Marie. She thus competed directly with the *Waubuno*, owned by the Beattys. Soon the two groups of owners combined, under the name of the Georgian Bay Navigation Company, to operate both vessels. In 1877 yet another competitor for the local trade, the *Maganettawan*, was launched at Byng Inlet. In November, 1879, the *Waubuno* was lost in a snowstorm with all of the twenty-four persons on board. The impact of the disaster was deeply felt both in Collingwood, where most of her crew had their homes, and in Parry Sound and along the North Shore, the destinations of her passengers.

In 1853 when William H. G. Kingston and his wife rattled over the rough Coldwater Road in the stage taking them to the dock at Sturgeon Bay, one of their fellow-passengers was a young woman, "dressed as a somewhat fine housemaid in England would be." She, with her baby, had been visiting relatives near Toronto. When they boarded the steamer *Kaloolah*, the steward told her that her husband was on board. Kingston was intrigued when the husband turned out to be ". . . a very superior and interesting Indian of the name of George, [who] . . . wore a shooting-jacket and round hat, and looked like a superior mechanic." George had been educated by a missionary at Manitowaning, on Manitoulin Island; his wife had been a servant in the missionary's house. He had saved money; now he wanted to become a chief and found his own village. The whole of Manitoulin Island was then an Indian reservation, so he had established himself and a number of his relatives in a settlement to the west of Manitowaning at a place where the steamer passed through a narrow channel, and where it could conveniently stop to take on wood for fuel.

This was the beginning of Little Current. When the passengers on the *Kaloolah* arrived there, after their voyage around Georgian Bay, they found a wooded point that had been partly cleared of trees, with cord wood piled ready for the steamer. Close to the water, a little farther on, were six birch-bark wigwams, and a large shanty that belonged to George. (He was also constructing a small log house for the coming winter and intended in time to build a larger house on the hill above.) Kingston reported:

> George has chosen his settlement with good taste and judgement. . . . He proposes to open a store here, and will find voyageurs, woodcutters, and Indians his customers. He has engaged, also, to supply the steamer with wood; and as his people are expert fishermen and fish swarm in the neighbourhood, while by salting them he will have a certain market with the fish-dealers who come round on purpose to buy from the Indians, I see a fair prospect of his becoming a wealthy man.

George Obbotossaway and his wife, Sarah Newman, did not prosper so easily. In 1857 the Hudson's Bay Company opened a post at Little Current, and began to compete with George, not only in selling goods to the Indians, but also in selling wood to the steamer. With the assistance of the Indian agent, Captain Ironside, the Company bought from an Indian some improved land and an Indian log house; it also cut down a quantity of wood. In doing these things it considerably exceeded its authority, which was merely to establish the store, and it did not bother to pay the Indians for the wood that had been cut. All of these events took place shortly before the arrival of two special Commissioners who had been appointed the preceding year by the Legislature to investigate Indian affairs. They discovered that the Indians of Manitoulin Island and both the Protestant and Catholic missionaries there were complaining loudly about the Company's activities. Those activities were stopped forthwith, and as a result of the Commissioners' report the Company lost its licence to trade on the island the following January.

The Hudson's Bay Company departed, but it left behind it a dock that it had built. This construction had been within the bounds of the permission given it, and so it asked for compensation. The Indian department after some thought decided that the dock would be valuable to the Indians, and in 1859 it authorized the sale of wood from Indian lands to the steamer in order to pay for the purchase. Captain Ironside, who had been considerably embarrassed by the commotion over the Hudson's Bay Company activities that he had abetted, waited until George had cut down and stacked his wood (and had paid the woodcutters in goods from his store) and then seized all that was cut. George, who by this time was living in his own frame house, undoubtedly had been one of those who complained most loudly about the Company; it is hard not to suppose that Ironside was taking revenge against a trouble-maker. The Rev. James Chance, a missionary who visited Little Current not long after the event, wrote a strong letter of protest. George himself wrote to the Sheriff at Sault Ste. Marie. The Indian department, however, stood behind the agent, saying that the wood was the property of all of the Indians, and therefore it was correct to use it in the manner that would most benefit all of them.

In August of 1861 the Commissioner of Crown Lands reported that the scheme of settling Indians on the island was a failure, for only 1,250 of them were then living there, and suggested that the agreements for the Indians could be observed merely by giving them small amounts of land for their houses. The white man was closing in on Manitoulin Island. That October two officials called upon the Indians at Mani-towaning with the proposition that they settle for 25 acres each. The Indians refused to accept the offer and also refused to permit a survey of the land.

In 1862 William McDougall, Superintendent-General of Indian Affairs, came to Manitowaning himself, with an offer of 100 acres for each Indian family and 50 acres for each single person, the proceeds from sales of the remaining land to be put in a fund for the benefit of the Indians—after deducting the expenses of surveys and administration. He paid out on the spot $700 in small amounts to various Indians to sweeten the offer. The Indians of Wikwemikong vigorously opposed ceding the land, however, and the discussion finally reached a stalemate on a Saturday night. Next morning, while the Wikwemikong Indians were at church, McDougall signed up all of the chiefs representing tribes living west of Manitowaning Bay and South Bay.

The missionaries at Wikwemikong were outraged, and charged that McDougall used false promises, threats, and whiskey to achieve his ends. But on Tuesday, October 6th, 1862, a final treaty was signed ceding everything on the island west of the two bays. Those Indians of Wikwemikong who had agreed to the treaty were expelled from their reservation by the other members of their tribe. During 1863 and 1864 there was much agitation on the part of the missionaries to have the treaty annulled. In 1863 the authorities feared an uprising and landed twenty-two armed policemen on Manitoulin. The force arrested a chief and started to handcuff one of the missionaries. The Indians reacted so violently that the invaders agreed to a truce, if the "offending parties" would go to Quebec to discuss matters and try to settle them.

Despite all attempts to delay the inevitable, it happened in April 1866: Manitoulin Island was opened to settlement at a price of fifty cents per acre, payable in advance. By 1870 it was fairly well settled. Between 1872 and 1880 its population grew by 15,000 people, largely drawn there by lumbering. And by 1890 there were three large mills at Little Current. The expansion of George's cordwood business had been phenomenal; but he had not profited greatly by it.

Near the southeastern corner of Georgian Bay a few miles east of Penetanguishene is a deep natural harbour protected against all winds. On the charts it was called Christendom Bay; locally it was known as Mundy's Bay. The land of Asher Mundy, tavernkeeper at the old naval and military establishment at Penetanguishene, had extended almost to the shore of this bay and he had cleared a portage through to the water. In the autumn of the year 1871 there were five log shanties through the surrounding bush, each with its own bleak little clearing. There was also a single frame building of larger size, built the preceding summer by Thomas Gladstane, who had come there with his family to open a store.

The Gladstane family reached their new home in November. Eight days later a group of directors of the Midland Railway arrived to inspect the place that had been selected as the Georgian Bay terminus of their road. There being no place else, they stayed with the Gladstanes. Among them was Baron Adolphus von Hugel, who had drawn a great deal of German money into the railway company. There was some discussion about a name for the new town that would rise on Mundy's Bay and the Baron suggested that it be named after the railway itself. Midland it became.

The next year the town began to take shape. In the spring a party of surveyors arrived to lay out streets and lots. The first sawmill was completed a little later that year, and both a telegraph office and a post office were established. An old resident has described the way things looked five years later:

> Slab Town was separated from "Up-Town" by saw-dust piles, and a swamp, no sidewalks and no real road, only as it happened to be passable accordingly as the weather was wet or dry or if the snow wasn't too deep and badly drifted. "Up-Town" was no better . . . no side-walks, no street lights and no anything, but a few straggling frame buildings, and the residence part of the place was in harmony, and had a few scattering houses two or three blocks away from the post office on streets running the same direction as Main Street. . . .
>
> At the time of which I am writing or from about 1875 until 1877 Slab Town consisted in addition to the big saw mill and the office, the boarding house, on the corner near the office, and about a dozen houses put up roughly from un-planed lumber, some of them on a street facing the lumber piles and saw-mill and others in the rear of these. . . .

The town's amusements had a genuinely homespun quality. When the town policeman married, someone dropped salt about his house, so that all of the village cows assembled there that night, with bells clanking. They came back the second night, too. Most people kept animals that wandered freely; a Mrs. Deschanes, who lived near the mills in Slabtown, owned a flock of geese. Pranksters fed the geese some wheat that had been soaked in whiskey and were gratified to see them stagger for a while and then collapse. Their owner came home to discover them sprawled out on the ground, and she decided that they had been poisoned. To keep them from becoming a total loss she immediately set to work and plucked the feathers. By the time the last bird had been plucked they had all begun to sober up and walk around, and she found herself with a live flock of naked geese.

In 1879, John Dollar, a young man from Scotland, built a mill just east of Midland in what became known as Dollartown (and also became known as the local resort of loggers in from the woods). Dollar lived in Midland on Hugel Avenue, one of the better residential streets. The first Presbyterian church in town was completed the year that he arrived, and finding the streets too muddy for the Sunday-morning walk, he had a board sidewalk built from his home to the church. He left Midland in 1890 for what proved to be considerably greener fields; the Dollar family attainments in Pacific coast shipping are much better known than their early history on Georgian Bay.

The British-American Lumber Company in 1881 constructed the first electric light plant to be put into permanent operation in Canada and illuminated its mill and yards with arc lamps; this was so wonderful that excursion trains and steamers brought people to Midland to see it. At about the same time the company installed a telephone system linking its plants and office. That year the railway began to erect the first wooden grain elevator on the harbour front. The town had several hotels, a saloon, a number of general stores and small shops, and a boat-building plant. The harbour attracted both passenger and freight vessels. It also sheltered a fleet of Mackinaw fishing boats.

The railway and the port of Midland were a productive combination. The mills at Midland, which quickly used up all of the local forests, could draw, for a time almost without competition, on much of the Muskoka area and the North Shore up to Parry Sound. The railway gave them one great advantage over the lumber operations based at Parry Sound and Byng Inlet: from Midland they could ship by rail to Lake Ontario and thence to the New York market as well as directly by water to the Chicago market. Therefore they could afford to reach past their competitors to the north and to bring logs down by water in great rafts from the entire North Shore, afterward shipping the finished products to the best markets. In order to reach the eastern consumers the mills of the North Shore had to ship finished lumber by water to Midland and there transfer it to the railway. Midland by 1890 had a population of about 3,000, the greater part of whom depended in some way on the lumber industry.

Rail lines spread all around Georgian Bay, except at the extreme northern end. The Northern Railway was extended to Meaford in 1872, and the narrow gauge Toronto, Grey and Bruce reached Owen Sound from Toronto in 1873. In 1882 the first rail line came to Wiarton, at the base of the Bruce Peninsula, and during the six to eight months of the summer season, twenty-five carloads a day of lumber and wood products were shipped out of that town alone, sometimes with as many as three locomotives to a train struggling to pull it up the hill leading from the business district. In 1897 the Ottawa, Arnprior and Parry Sound Railway reached its terminus at Depot Harbour, five miles from Parry Sound. John R. Booth, the Ottawa lumber king who built the line, thought the Parry Sounders put too high a price on their land when he wanted to buy there and so he built his own port; but the effect was the same and Parry Sound had access to the shortest road from Georgian Bay to Montreal and the New England coast.

All of the mill towns continued to boom. Logs came down from Manitoulin Island to Wiarton, Owen Sound, and Collingwood, and from the North Shore rivers, which drew on a wide hinterland, to Parry Sound and Midland. In 1900 the amount of lumber produced at Midland was second only to Ottawa in all of Canada.

By 1900 most of the forests that were to be seen fifty years before on the shores of Georgian Bay had disappeared, to be replaced in part by farm land, but in larger part by slashed-over terrain where the scars healed only gradually as second growth trees emerged. Instead of the two small towns of Pene-tanguishene and Sydenham there were at least ten vigorous centres where smoke and steam rose above the mills and the factories of wood products. All but a few of these places were connected by rail to the older Canadian cities and thence in some manner to the American east coast. All of them were connected by water to the American cities on Lakes Erie, Huron, and Michigan, and especially to Chicago. There were grain elevators at several Bay ports and the grain trade from the west was beginning to bring wheat from the prairies to be transferred to railways at points on Georgian Bay and there sent east. Shipyards had grown in Owen Sound and Colling-wood and small vessels were built at almost every port. In a scant half-century Georgian Bay had changed entirely.

# The falling of the pine

*Come all young men a-wanting of courage bold undaunted,*
*Repair unto the shanties before your youth's decline.*
*The spectators they will ponder and gaze on you with wonder,*
*For your noise exceeds the thunder in the falling of the pine.*

So sang the early loggers on Georgian Bay; the song was evidently written by someone with a literary turn of mind and then severely battered during constant repetition in the logging camps.

Probably most of the loggers who first came to Collingwood after 1855 on the new railway and spread out from there over the Bay were Canadians. It was not until the 80's that the woods of Georgian Bay became as familiar to American loggers as the woods of Michigan. Throughout the Canadian lumber industry the French were still the largest single group. The French were also the most gaily dressed, with red or multicoloured sashes and long, pointed red *toques* on their heads, in addition to the general uniform of spiked boots, grey trousers, two flannel shirts (worn at the same time), and a blanket coat that later became known around the Great Lakes as a mackinaw.

These woodsmen were not greatly different from the men who had made past history on Georgian Bay. The French were the descendents of the *voyageurs*. The others were scarcely a generation removed from the pioneers. All were used to hard living and a scant income.

The shanties in which the men lived were log buildings chinked with moss, with side walls six feet high and peaked roofs. They were temporary buildings, intended for use only as long as the trees lasted in their vicinity, and they were not put together with studied care. They varied in size, the largest being perhaps 35 by 40 feet. Inside, the walls were lined with two tiers of bunks, made of balsam boughs laid on poles hewn flat on top. On one side of the building was space for grindstones, water barrels and a couple of wash basins, the cook's shelves and work table, the clerk's desk, and the van chest that held tobacco and clothing the men could buy. The van chest was also the camp drugstore, limited normally to liniment, laxatives, and sticking plaster. The foreman's bunk was usually separate in one corner. There was no limit to the number who could occupy the other bunks. The men all just piled in, head first and feet towards the fire, taking off only their boots or the moccasins they wore around camp, sometimes having to roll over in unison when the fit was really tight. A bench made from a half log with the flat side up or from a squared log, held on blocks or legs, ran along in front of the bunks. The English-speaking men called it the deacon's seat. The essential part of the whole shanty, of course, was space for bunks; the amount of room allowed for the frills depended on the size of the building.

In the middle of the shanty was a square of logs about twelve feet to a side, holding a foot of earth, where a fire burned day and night. Four posts rose from the corners to the roof, and cooking pots were hung over the fire by an adjustable crane fixed to one of them. Overhead there was a large hole in the roof to let smoke out and air in. Above the hole was a big squat chimney made of logs.

Usually the men were asleep by eight or nine at night. The cook was up between three and four in the morning; it was one of his duties to wake the others. The classic reveille call was "Day-light in the swamp!" and the cook sounded off with it at the top of his voice between four and five. Imaginative cooks made up their own morning calls which were more original but less printable.

The breakfast that followed usually consisted of baked beans, bread, and strong tea. (Some camps charged a man $1.00 a month for the tea.) Tin plates, cups or basins, and spoons were provided by the camp; each man bought himself a small butcher knife that he used as both knife and fork. Only the men who worked close to camp would come in for the noon meal; the others might carry food or it might be sent out to them. Supper was the big feed. Salt pork, pea soup, bread, and potatoes were the staples. The better camps, especially in later years, might sometimes have boiled beef instead of the pork, and provide a dessert made of rice and raisins or dried apples. Meals were eaten in absolute silence for reasons that are obscure; the rule was enforced by the cook. As a result of the diet, some loggers by spring would be laid up with what the men called "black leg"—a form of scurvy—and others would be affected by night blindness and have to be led back to camp once the sun went down. These ailments seem to have been accepted as normal hazards of the life.

Loggers didn't bathe and had uncouth manners, but usually they were honest and generous. The Cook Brothers at one time had a particularly large camp in the northern part of the Bruce Peninsula, with a big shanty that housed a crew of eighty-two men. Alexander Gilchrist, a local settler, contracted to manage the camp. On one occasion Gilchrist, using his own team, was drawing logs across Gillies Lake on the ice and down to the Bay shore. The ice on the small lake broke; the horses fell through and were drowned. The Cooks refused to pay Gilchrist for his loss, whereupon the eighty-two loggers—men whose pay might average sixteen dollars a month—passed the hat and collected enough to buy a new team.

The loggers attacked the pine in the interest of two separate trades. The first and oldest of these was the preparation of squared timbers for shipment to Quebec and thence to England. The export of timbers from Canada had first gained impetus when Napoleon cut the British off from the Baltic, and it had developed ever since. By 1825 rafts of squared timbers were being sent down the St. Lawrence from Lake Ontario. By the 1850's the forests on the northern shores of Lake Ontario were getting sparse; the railway came to Georgian Bay at a strategic moment. Some loads of squared timber probably went by schooner before the Northern Railway arrived at Collingwood, but that development marked the real beginning of timber shipments to places distant from the Bay.

The Canadian trade in sawed lumber, as opposed to squared timber, was at first the result of demands from the eastern United States, particularly New York. By the 1850's New York State was at the height of its lumber manufacturing period, but white pine had been used up in most of the New England states, and lumber operators had been gradually moving west to Michigan and north to Canada. Occasional lumber cargoes must have gone out of Georgian Bay on schooners before 1855, but the completion of the railway to the Bay came just as the lumber industry was looking for new timber limits, and the export of lumber in quantity dates from about that year.

After the arrival of the railway a large saw mill was built in Collingwood by the S. C. Kennedy Company. It was known locally as the Big Red Mill. The Company obtained rights to the forests along the Nottawasaga, east of Collingwood, and began sending logs down the river. Log rafts were made up on the Nottawasaga and then towed to Collingwood by tugs. At first the tugs were able to go some distance up river; then over a period of years the cutting of trees caused the river to fall, so that towards the end of the logging operations tugs had to wait in the Bay, outside the river mouth, and the rafts were brought out to them.

The railway not only began a flow of timber and lumber eastward, but it also stimulated much other activity. The steamers that were placed on the Collingwood-Chicago run as soon as the railway was completed carried lumber and wood products among other cargoes for Chicago. Once the lumbermen started on the Bay shore they soon outran the rails and were hard at work in many places from which they could only ship by water.

Immediately to the west of Collingwood the area was settled, and all of the pineries there consisted of small private holdings interspersed with expanding farm lands. The large-scale logging methods of the big operators did not fit into such a countryside. The private owners would cut their trees when they wished, and would sell them in their own good time either to the big companies or to small mills for local use. Moving west and north past Collingwood and Owen Sound, however, one comes to the Bruce Peninsula. There the lands were opened for settlement in 1856; and there the government tried to get double return for its Indian wards by selling to different people the timber rights and the settlement rights for the same land. The well-established firm of Cook Brothers bought the timber licences and began to cut trees for squared timbers in 1863. The settlers bought the land. For the next twenty years the Cooks logged the Bruce and the logging blighted settlement.

Logging operations were also carried on to the east of Collingwood, beyond the Nottawasaga. Most of the men who bought the limits in this direction were more interested in the production of lumber than of squared timber.

By 1874 there were seven mills in the Georgian Bay area that were important enough to be mentioned in the American publication, the *Lumberman's Gazette*. Among them were mills at Spanish River, Byng Inlet, Sturgeon Bay, and Waubaushene. Between 1870 and 1880 the population of Manitoulin Island increased by 15,000, drawn there largely by lumbering. The Bay was starting to boom.

The yearly cycle of logging was as unvaried as the seasons it followed. In the autumn before snow fell, trees were cut, roads were made, and streams were prepared for the spring drive; during the winter the felling of trees continued and logs were hauled to the edge of the water and piled in dumps; in the spring they were rolled into the streams and taken to the Bay.

The most dramatic part of the yearly cycle was the spring drive. Logs, stamped on the ends with their owner's marks, were rolled into streams when the spring floods were at their height, to be carried down by swift currents. Loggers, stationed along the banks or riding in pointers (*bateaux* with long stems which enabled them to ride up over logs), herded them along, watching particularly that none of them lodge behind a rock, for that might start a jam. Good white-water men could also ride on the logs themselves, jumping from log to log, digging in the spikes on their boots and depending on their sense of balance. The cook and his cooking outfit travelled along in another pointer and set up periodically on the shore. Usually there were four meals a day when the drive was on.

Jams were the chief fear of river drivers, and as logging moved farther back from the North Shore and the drives became longer—eventually as much as 300 miles up the winding rivers—the chances for a jam increased. Once a jam formed, volunteers had to go out on the packed logs and cut or move the key log, hoping that they could scramble ashore or ride to safety as the jam freed. The perils of this job are celebrated in numerous logger songs and stories that tell of heroes killed when jams broke.

One of these was Sandy Gray, boss of a river-driving gang on the Musquosh, who gave his name to Sandy Gray Falls. Sandy was the fair-haired blacksheep of a pious Victorian family and was admired by lumbermen as an outstanding reprobate. On a Sunday morning in June 1867, he proved it. There was a log jam at the top of the falls that morning and Sandy, ignoring the Sabbath, avowed to his men, "Boys, we'll break the jam or breakfast in hell," and set to work. Some people say that he cut the key log with an axe and some that he moved it with a cant hook, but in any event the vengeful God of his ancestors took direct action: the jam freed so quickly that it carried him over the falls.

Once they got the logs to a saw mill town or a harbour, the loggers turned to other things. They patronized tailors and jewellers heavily, but these merchants were secondary attractions. Having been many months in the bush, the loggers were bushed, and they set about relieving that condition. Sir Richard Bonnycastle in 1846 described the interests of lumberjacks at Quebec as the fiddle, the female, and the fire-water. Stewart Holbrook listed the recreations of loggers at Saginaw as booze, bawds, and battle. Over a span of a half century and the

*Samuel de Champlain sent the first explorers and missionaries to Georgian Bay and visited the area himself in 1615.*

*Etienne Brulé, the first white man to see Georgian Bay, arrived there in 1610.*

The big canoes of the fur trade companies came down the French River in spring on the long voyage from Montreal to the west.

Gone is the wilderness and the threat of Indian attack, but Fort Sainte Marie, reconstructed, looks very much as it did in 1640.

Penetanguishene in 1818 was a small but strategic naval establishment hugging the shores of a harbour that provided shelter for many vessels.

St. James-on-the-Lines, an Anglican church built for the garrison at Penetanguishene in 1838, is still standing and in use today.

The British schooner Nancy *played a*
*prominent role in the War of 1812. She*
*was burned and sunk by the Americans*
*in 1814.*

*The figurehead of the* Nancy *has been*
*reconstructed from descriptions written*
*at the time the schooner was built.*

*In winter logs were drawn in sleds to the banks of nearby streams. When the ice broke in the spring they were floated down the rivers.*

Boats similar to those shown in this 1880 picture of the Collingwood fishing fleet came to be used all over the Bay and the Upper Lakes.

A freighter loads pulpwood from a boom in Gore Bay, Manitoulin.

*The S.S.* Kaloolah *ran from Sturgeon Bay to the Sault.*

*This ad appeared in 1879, the year the* Waubuno *sank.*

*The* Chicora, *a blockade runner, became a passenger ship.*

*The* Huronic *was the first steel ship built at Collingwood.*

LAKE SUPERIOR DIVISION
HURONIC
MAJESTIC
MONARCH
EMPIRE
HEAD OFFICE SARNIA, ONTARIO.

**THE NORTHERN NAVIGATION COMPANY**
OF ONTARIO, LIMITED.
THE GREAT LAKES ROUTE.

GEORGIAN BAY DIVI
CITY OF COLLINGWOOD
CITY OF MIDLAND
CITY OF TORONTO
ATLANTIC
BRITANNIC
GERMANIC
HEAD OFFICE COLLINGWOOD

# GEORGIAN BAY HOUSE,

## JOHN HOGAN, PROPRIETOR.
### PENETANGUISHENE, ONTARIO, CANADA.

The Georgian Bay House is one of the most comfortable and commodious hotels in the province. It has ample accommodation for two hundred guests. Its rooms are cool, airy and well apportioned, making a residence at this hotel delightful during the summer months. The table is replete with the best to be obtained, whilst the comfort and enjoyment of its guests is attended to by the personal supervision of the proprietor. For the summer tourist who seeks

**Lovely Scenery, Pure, Cool Breezes, Boating without Danger,**

the best fishing on the continent, the vicinity of Penetang fills the utmost requirements.

The town abounds in walks and drives amongst shady woods, and the boating in the harbour and outer bay is perfectly protected from storm or danger ; boating accidents are unknown.

## TERMS, from $1.00 to $2.50 per day, according to location of rooms.

AN EXCELLENT LIVERY. DRIVES AND PIC-NIC PARTIES ARRANGED FOR ON MODERATE TERMS.

*A summer hotel, advertised in an 1884 guidebook, offered Victorian luxury.*

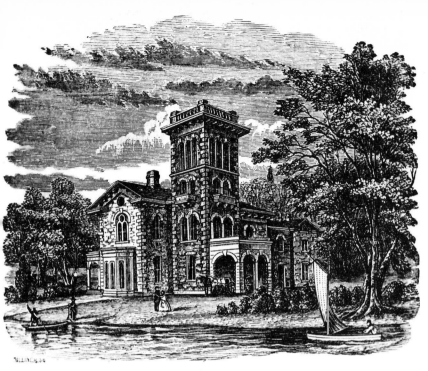

*The 1880 Georgian Bay "cottage" was apt to be an elaborate affair.
Its modern counterpart is less pretentious but much more comfortable.*

*The Thirty Thousand Islands is an ideal region for cruising, swimming, fishing and camping.*

*The Blue Mountains attract many winter vacationists and skiers.*

*Penetanguishene takes its name from an Indian word meaning "falling sand."*
*The modern town is very different from the 1818 community pictured earlier.*

*King Street in Midland runs directly to the harbour, a busy port well provided*
*with docks and grain elevators. The town is in the centre of a farming area.*

From the Collingwood Shipyards come many of the freighters on the Lakes.

The people of the Georgian Bay region value the past but look to the present as well. Their factories produce a wide variety of goods: electric heaters, furniture (made from logs like those being unloaded here) and pottery made from local clay.

The Martyrs' Shrine looks down on the walls and the towers of Sainte Marie.

*Georgian Bay has a tremendous appeal to many people who take pleasure in the scenic grandeur of the rocky islands, rugged shores and wide expanses of water.*

distance from Quebec to Saginaw, the men changed little. On Georgian Bay they headed for those places where a relaxed atmosphere prevailed, such as Dollartown at Midland and Parry Harbour at Parry Sound—which was known to all loggers as "Parry Hoot." The noises of revelry and fighting that drifted out of those resorts might keep some people awake in the more sedate parts of town, but most of the citizens who lived around the Bay were used to them.

The bosses had better living conditions than their men, but they still had to be pretty tough. By 1878 Robert Dollar, John's brother who had come with him from Scotland, had married and was living at Bracebridge. He had gone into partnership with Hiram Cook and had lumber camps scattered through Muskoka and along the North Shore of the Bay; one of them was on a sizeable island near Parry Sound. For that one, the equipment, men, horses, and provisions that were to last until spring were all put on a steamer, carried to the island, and unloaded there. Early the next March a letter, which had been carried across the ice by an Indian, came to Dollar from the foreman. It said that the camp was running short of fodder for the horses, and that unless some was sent in to them, the animals would starve before the opening of navigation.

It was a bad situation. The ice might start to break up at any time, but vessels would not be able to move on the Bay for a couple of months. Dollar went to Midland, bought four loads of feed, and hired four teams of horses to pull the loads across the ice. To get the use of the horses, he had to guarantee that if they were drowned the owners would be repaid. With the four loads and a small group of men, he started out on March 20th, bridging over the occasional cracks they encountered in the ice, steering by compass and a chart. About three in the afternoon snow began to fall and then a heavy gale hit without warning, blowing one team off its feet. By the time they got the horses up again, the wind was blowing so hard and there was so much snow that they couldn't go on. They formed the loads into a hollow square for protection and put men and horses inside the square. The soft wet snow had soaked everyone and it did not seem possible that they could live through the night on the open Bay in the extreme cold.

Dollar saw on his chart that there was a small island directly to windward. It might provide shelter. Taking an axe, he started in its direction, but he had gone no more than a quarter of a mile when he found that the wind was so strong and the snow choked him so much that he was not able to continue. He had gone directly into the wind; he returned with the wind at his back. When he had gone far enough to reach his starting point he still could see nothing. He lay down on the ice and called, hoping that the men would hear him, but when he tried to raise his voice he choked on the hard-driven snow and could make little noise. He got up and started again. Finally he realized that the wind had shifted and that he now had no idea where he was.

He went on, over places where the ice was covered by water, his clothing frozen solid, falling, breaking a hand—although he did not at the time know it—and at last falling and striking the back of his head. He lay unconscious for a while until the snow on his face revived him. Then he raised himself on an elbow and saw land fifty feet away.

> I immediately felt as if there was nothing wrong with me, and jumped up as smart as I ever did in my life. Although it was a barren, inhospitable shore—no habitation within fifty miles of me—I was well pleased with it. I walked into the woods far enough to get out of the wind and cut a lot of wood (I never had let go of my ax) and lit a fire. My clothes were frozen so stiff it was only with great difficulty I was able to get my hands into my pocket. When I got out my match box there were only two left in it. I need not say that I took great precautions to make sure they would not miss fire. I got behind a perpendicular rock out of the wind, and everything ready, was pleased beyond measure when the first match started the fire. My anxiety was great as it would have been impossible to have survived, wet as I was, through the intense cold of that night. I kept a good fire going and got my clothes thawed out and dried, but did not sleep any. At daybreak I started back to the ice, and found it calm and a clear, bright morning.

Convinced that the rest of his party were dead, he started back towards the place he thought he might find them. Every so often he saw his own tracks and from them learned that he had gone for over three miles parallel to the shore, never more than five hundred feet away from it. After he had walked eight or ten miles he saw the horses a long way off on the horizon. He walked quickly to reach them and in time the men saw him. They had survived by making a fire, using as fuel most of one load of the fodder. The men were overjoyed at his reappearance, for they had been certain he was dead and did not think they could get home without having him to guide them. During the night they had lost their provisions and the only thing they had to eat was bran mash, without salt. It was about noon when he joined them, so they made a fire and each one had a share of the bran mash.

The men wanted to head back to Midland but he persuaded them to go on. That night they camped on a small island in thick woods. The following night after dark they came to the island where the lumber camp was located. Snow had been falling all day, and it was a Sunday, so the loggers had not been outside the shanty and there were no tracks to guide the new arrivals; but after considerable searching they finally located the camp.

> Next morning I could not move in my bed. I never was so sore in my life. The teams had to return at once as the ice gave signs of breaking up. I called the teamsters to my bed and told them we would send an Indian guide who would take them back as I would have to stay until I got better. They positively refused to go without me, so I got some of them to rub me to get me limbered up, but it was a terrible job to get out of bed. However, we got started, and got through all right except getting the horses in the water several times.

The experience did nothing to slow Dollar down. He continued to establish camps along the North Shore. In 1881 in the early spring he started to return with a sled and team over the ice from a camp on Serpent River, on the North Channel, where his men were cutting squared timbers for the English market. With him he brought a dozen loggers who would not be needed at that camp for the spring drive. By the time they reached Little Current the ice had melted so that it would not support the sled and team. Dollar had to go on, for his business was pressing, but he tried to get the men to return. They were as eager to reach the delights of civilization as he was to get to his business however, so he bought some hand sleighs from the Indians and he and the men continued on foot, pulling the sleighs.

On the fourth morning out, after a severe storm, they woke to find the ice had gone. They proceeded to work their way through the forest to French River, only to discover that the ice had gone from the river as well. They made a raft of logs; it capsized; they made a bigger one. It got them across. On the far side they saw that ice still remained between the islands and the shore. Travelling over ice was much quicker than going through the bush and so they went on over the Bay, although during the afternoons the ice became so rotten that several men went through and all of them were constantly wet. They ran out of food and went hungry for some time. Ten miles north of Byng Inlet they found an Indian woman and two children camped on the shore. She made them flapjacks and cooked a three-foot-long whitefish by putting it in a pot of boiling water, "scales, guts and all."

That night they reached Byng Inlet. Dollar sent an Indian back with supplies for the woman, to repay her several times over; then next morning he started out on snowshoes to his camp at Shawanaga, forty-five miles away. There they were getting out logs that were to be towed across the Bay and Lake Huron to Detroit. He completed his business in the forenoon and was taken by team to Rosseau, arriving after midnight; from there he walked thirty-five miles to his headquarters at Bracebridge, and next morning was busy hiring men for the spring drives at his various camps.

In the early 80's the demand for lumber caused by settlement in the western states began to increase rapidly. The big mills at Saginaw and other Michigan cities had used up most

of the Michigan forests and the mill owners had to look farther afield to get their logs. In 1886 two companies started
carrying them from the North Shore of the Bay to Michigan
in barges, the largest of which was 271 feet long. This operation lasted only during that summer, however, for the barges
proved too expensive for the job. The American lumbermen
then began instead to raft their logs across Georgian Bay and
Lake Huron, using bag-booms: strings of logs, chained together end to end, that completely circled a large number of
other logs which floated inside the bag. The booms were
towed by tugs.

The rafts were not beloved of Lake sailors. The largest of
them covered an area on the water of well over twenty-five
acres. They moved along at a speed of one mile an hour,
towed by one, two, or three tugs, according to their size. In a
storm they might get completely out of control and drag the
tugs way off course. They carried away buoys and forced
steamers aground in narrow waters; steamers collided with
them in open waters, particularly in fog or at night when
they often were poorly lighted. The shipowners pushed re-
strictive legislation on rafting through the United States House
of Representatives; the raftsmen mobilized their strength in the
Senate and defeated it.

During the 90's the people of Georgian Bay watched with
growing indignation as their forests went rafting away to the
States. The Bay was unhappily close to being a one-industry
region, and that industry, the production of lumber, depended
on the forests that were being taken elsewhere. Few people at
that time had any thought of conservation, but logs that went
to Michigan were not sawed in Georgian Bay mills, by
Georgian Bay labour, to the profit of Georgian Bay companies.

The period from 1890 to 1898 was marked by increasing
manœuvres between American and Canadian lumbermen to
get their respective governments to help them out. In 1897 the
United States placed a tariff on Canadian lumber, but not on
Canadian logs. The new law, known as the Dingley Bill, also
provided that if any country put an export duty on the products it sent the United States, retaliatory measures could be
taken. It seemed that most of the Georgian Bay mills were

doomed, for their primary markets were now cut off. The American lumbermen appeared to have won the battle entirely.

The Canadian government, fearing retaliatory action, would do nothing. The Ontario legislature, however, came to the rescue. The timber limits that were being cut by the American companies were on Crown lands. The companies had bought the use of land within particular limits, but Ontario kept titles to this property. In 1898 the legislature passed an act requiring that all logs cut on government lands be further manufactured within Ontario. This was not a duty, but the regulation of a landowner regarding his own property, and so the retaliatory clauses of the United States tariff law did not apply. The Michigan lumbermen cried breach of contract. The Ontario government replied that the licences were only for one year and if the Michiganers wanted to renew the next year they would have to abide by the rule.

This act effectively killed the export of logs and with it the whole American log-rafting industry. Promptly a number of United States companies established their own mills in the Georgian Bay region. Lumber went streaming out of the Bay towns more quickly than ever by rail and water, mainly to American markets.

Perhaps the most novel example of this is the case of a Michigan lumberman who stole his own mill and carried it bodily to the North Channel, where he reassembled it. It was a recently-built mill at Saginaw, and was about to fail because of the added expense of logs now that the new Ontario regulation was in effect. Creditors had already stationed watchmen at the mill. One night a bottle of whiskey was left where one watchman could find it, and the other man was called away on a false emergency. A short time later, two tugs and two lighters drew in to the mill, where the machinery had already been dismantled behind locked doors. The machinery and everything else—even the siding of the building and the nails that held it on—were loaded on the lighters, and the tugs and lighters departed next morning at half past one. During the following day the Sheriff of Sault Ste. Marie, Michigan, located them, stuck in the ice, in Canadian waters near St.

Joseph Island. They were across the international boundary and one of the mill owners threatened him with a rifle, so the officer went home. After the wind shifted and the ice broke, the tugs and lighters moved down the North Channel, finally coming to Moiles Harbour on John Island, about midway in the Channel. There the mill was assembled again and there it sawed logs for a number of years.

There is no accurate record of the number of mills that operated on Georgian Bay. One old-timer recalled that on the Bruce alone there were eight large mills near the town of Wiarton, plus some thirty smaller ones throughout the peninsula. They appeared like mushrooms in the middle of the forests, ate up the trees, and then disappeared themselves. Thus the formal tables of figures that purport to show how many board feet were produced each year are highly suspect. When they speak of particular mills or certain towns they might be fairly accurate, but just who was there to measure the output of every single mill? It is safe to say only that about 1900 the lumber boom on the Bay was at its height and that by 1905 it was beginning to diminish. During this period, Midland was the biggest lumber town. James Playfair, a Scottish-Canadian with an acutely developed business sense, came there in 1883 and grew to be one of the lumber princes of Georgian Bay. But in 1916 he formed a shipbuilding company in Midland, which purchased his largest mill, tore it down, and erected a shipyard where it had stood. This action is significant. The lumber industry faltered on—one historian says it died on the Bay in 1940—but the big money was long since gone. The small mills that now remain have more in common with the local mills that first appeared on the Bay than with the big operations of the boom years.

Lumber rocketed Georgian Bay into the twentieth century, lifted it to the heights of a great boom, and departed, never to return in the same form. The big forests were gone; the big mills torn down, or burned down, or fallen down; and the Bay region was left with an economic hangover that has not been fully cured to this day.

# Canoes, sails, and fishing craft

The canoe was the first craft to navigate Georgian Bay, and it has been in use there longer than any other carrier. Indians were using bark canoes when the French arrived; the French adopted them; and the British trading companies and government took them over. At least one attempt was made, in the iron canoe of Penetanguishene, to utilize a material that was more durable than bark. When bark finally became scarce the white man substituted cloth. Now aircraft manufacturers make canoes of light alloy, and others use fibreglass. Today the canoe is mainly a pleasure craft; it is well adapted to the inlets, rivers, and inland lakes along the North Shore; and it still is much used there.

One of the best early descriptions of Huron canoes was given by Brother Gabriel Sagard, who made the forty-day canoe trip to Georgian Bay in 1624. Sagard wrote:

> Their canoes are from eight to nine paces in length and about a pace and a half wide at the middle, tapering off to both ends like a weaver's shuttle, and these are the largest they make. They have also others smaller which they use as occasion requires and according to the difficulty of the journeys they have to make. The canoes are liable

to turn over if one does not understand how to manage them, being made of birch-bark strengthened within by little hoops of white cedar, very neatly placed, and they are so light that a man can easily carry one on his head or on his shoulder. Each can support the weight of a hogs head, more or less according to size.

We know little more than that about the canoes of the Hurons. The different tribes, living under different conditions, produced bark craft that resembled each other generally but that varied considerably in their details. The early destruction of the Huron culture has left us with little exact knowledge of their canoes.

As the French traders and later the British trading companies made their own canoes they combined, standardized, and modified the styles used by various tribes. The high-ended Algonquin canoes seem to have provided the basic model. All of the later trading-company canoes had high ends, so that when they were carried ashore and overturned, they were held at such an angle that they became shelters under which their crews could sleep. Although canoe factories were established in several places—the oldest being at Three Rivers, Quebec—their products were never standardized in the manner of a modern builder of stock boats. Certain classifications of canoes did become common, however, especially the *canôts du maitre*, big 35- to 40-footers, such as Sir John Franklin took from Penetanguishene to the head of Lake Superior, and the *canôts du nord*, about 25 feet long, which were used commonly by the government services and the traders on Georgian Bay. Between the two sizes there was an odd size with an obvious name, the *batard* canoe. There were also smaller types. These classifications were a matter of general custom only, and there was a good deal of variation.

Canoes were frequently painted in bright colours and those of the Hudson's Bay Company usually had the Company's flag—a British red ensign with the white letters HBC in the fly—painted on the stern. The initials, according to some, meant "Here Before Christ."

The big canoes were manned by *voyageurs* during both the

French and British periods, as the French names indicate. They also passed into French-Canadian folklore. Louis Frechette described the apparition of the *chasse-galerie* in this way: "It was something like a canoe, which travelled, rapidly as an arow, at about five hundred feet above the earth, manned by a dozen reprobates in red flannel shirts, paddling like damnation, with Satan standing in the stern, steering straight forward in the direction of Three Rivers."

The next craft to appear was the *bateau*, the flat-bottomed, round-sided, double-ended boat used by the armed forces and the trading companies alike. Some time before the War of 1812 it came into use on Georgian Bay. It was clumsier than a canoe and much harder to portage. Like the canoe it could be sailed before the wind with a simple rig. Its great advantages seem to have been that it could be built and operated by men who had ordinary sea-coast experience and skills, whereas it required specialists either to build or to paddle a canoe. In an emergency a *bateau* could be made from any kind of wood at any time of the year—unlike the canoe. It was also more durable than the canoe.

As the fur trade declined, many of the men engaged in it—or their sons—turned to lumbering. They took with them their old customs and equipment. As a result, both canoes and *bateaux* were used by the loggers. The canoes in time came to be restricted to the rivers and inland lakes, where their light weight was essential, and *bateaux* were normally employed in open waters. The lumberman's *bateau* was particularly suited to his needs, as we have seen; the long, sloping, pointed ends enabled it to run up on logs or log rafts. Since they were in everyday use in logging activities, *bateaux* remained available on the lumber coasts for general freight work of all kinds; they were in common use on the Bay until recent years and an occasional specimen may still be found.

The first true sailing vessel to come into Georgian Bay is a matter of conjecture; it could have been LaSalle's *Griffin*. The first known cargo vessels apparently were the *Nancy* and *Mink*, operating during the War of 1812. The first vessels built on

Georgian Bay were probably three small gunboats constructed at the naval establishment on the Nottawasaga in the spring of 1817 and named for local fauna: the *Bee*, the *Wasp*, and the *Mosquito*.

The first known wreck of Georgian Bay took place in 1828, when the Drummond Island garrison was transferred to Penetanguishene. The government chartered a brig and a schooner to carry soldiers, stores, and the belongings of government employees to the new station. They proved unable to do the job in the time allowed, and so William Solomon, Indian interpreter for the government, was told to arrange for the use of the schooner *Alice Hackett*, commanded by her owner, Captain Hackett. She had made at least one previous trip, carrying stores and people from Drummond Island.

This time she carried not only a detachment of soldiers and some military supplies, but also a man named Lepine with his wife and child, a tavern keeper named Frazer with his thirteen barrels of whiskey, and the belongings of William Solomon, among them considerable livestock and some household furniture. Solomon himself made the trip in another vessel with some of the officers and his family came in a *bateau*, coasting around the shore and camping at night.

After the *Alice Hackett* was a little way out from Drummond Island, Frazer, the tavern keeper, opened shop. Before long the captain and crew, and many of the soldiers, were in various stages of drunkenness. During the night a storm arose Those on the schooner were in no condition to think clearly and they let her run aground on Fitzwilliam Island, off the southern tip of Manitoulin Island.

The crew and most of the passengers made their way ashore. Of the cargo they saved only one horse, some pork, and the entire consignment of whiskey. Lepine's wife and the infant were left on the wreck and were not missed in the drunken confusion. The woman fastened the baby to her back and tied herself to the mast, where she remained throughout the storm. Next morning, the people on shore had become sober enough to realize that the woman and child were missing. They went out in the schooner's yawl boat, which had been saved, and took them to safety.

The schooner herself was a complete loss. Not only had the pounding on the shore damaged her, but a large cannon which had been travelling as deck cargo had come loose, fallen through a hatch, and gone completely through the bottom of the vessel. The horse remained on the island for several years and finally died there. As the result of all this, Fitzwilliam Island became known to mariners as Horse Island. Frazer and his thirteen barrels eventually reached Penetanguishene, where he established yet another tavern.

The first commercial sailing vessel of any consequence to be based on Georgian Bay after the War of 1812 was a schooner owned by Stephen Jeffery, who brought her to Penetang from Lake Ontario. It has been said that she was the *Annie and Jane*, of York, the first vessel to pass through the Welland Canal from Lake Ontario to Lake Erie on November 27th, 1829, but that seems unlikely. In any event, she arrived late in 1829 or early in 1830 and was soon at work carrying stone from Quarry Island to Penetanguishene for the new barracks there.

By 1845 there was a sloop that sailed regularly between Sturgeon Bay at the northern end of the Coldwater Road and Sydenham, with a stop at Penetanguishene, carrying both passengers and cargo. By 1850 it had been replaced by the steamer *Gore*.

One of the first commercial vessels built on Georgian Bay was the schooner *Ann Mackenzie*, about a hundred-footer, launched at Sydenham in 1848. One of the ship carpenters who built her, and who had not been paid, retained a lawyer some time later to find out where she had gone. It turned out she had been sent to Toronto, from where she had carried lumber to Quebec, had crossed the Atlantic to a British port, and had then sailed for Rio de Janeiro.

Probably the first three-master built on the Bay was the *Belle McPhee*. Launched at Sydenham as a two-masted schooner about 1850, she was overhauled after three years of service, had thirty feet added to her length—undoubtedly by splicing in a section amidships, which was the usual system— and was given a third mast. The following year she struck a rock off Thornbury and sank. Her crew was rescued by a fishing tug.

By the early 50's schooners were sailing fairly often from Toronto to Georgian Bay ports. Schooners were also beginning to take lumber to ports in the United States. At the beginning of steamship service from Collingwood to Chicago and Green Bay in 1855, cargoes of coal for the steamers began to arrive at Collingwood by sailing vessel. In 1856 two Canadian vessels, the barque *Malta* and the schooner *Carolina Marsh*, were chartered to run in connection with the railway. The *Malta* made the record passage from Chicago to Collingwood in July 1856, taking only fifty hours for the trip. That fall she took twenty-six days for the same passage in stormy weather and arrived at Collingwood having lost all of her sails, her large anchor, and 45 fathoms of anchor chain.

When the *Malta* was about to sail on one of her voyages to Chicago it developed that half of her crew were in the Collingwood jail. Her mate, with a few volunteers from other vessels, went to the court house and forced his way in. After a satisfying battle, in which a policeman was thrown through a window into the street, the sailors were assembled and taken back to their ship.

What today is the Midwestern United States was beginning to produce grain in quantity by the late 50's. From Michigan ports it went down the Lakes or went across them to Collingwood, where it was sent eastward by rail. Flour came also to Collingwood. By the early 80's grain was also coming in to Midland and Owen Sound. The grain trade drew a number of large sailing vessels, both American and Canadian, most of them three-masted schooners. A number of Canadian vessels came also in other trades. Most hailed from Lake Ontario ports and were designed so that they could pass through the Welland Canal; they could be no longer than 140 feet and usually were rather boxlike in their lines in order to provide the most cargo space possible for their length. The United States vessels, which normally sailed only on the Lakes above Niagara Falls and did not have to fit the canal, were both larger and more graceful. The biggest was about 200 feet long.

There also were many small schooners on the Bay. At a time when railroad lines were incomplete and eccentric, roads poor, and motor trucks unknown, the schooners went anywhere and carried anything. They took Georgian Bay grain from small ports near where it grew and added it to the volume passing through Collingwood. They carried other farm produce, supplies for the little isolated communities, fish, and cedar posts. Most of their work was beneficial, but some of it was not. At the end of November, 1864, the schooner *Stanley*, McNab master, of Owen Sound, brought whiskey to the Indians at Little Current and as a result there was a near-riot in the village.

One of these small carriers was the two-masted schooner *Otonabee*, which loaded lumber and shingles at Muskoka Mills, and then on November 5th, 1880 was towed by a tug as far as Giant's Tomb, where open water begins. She anchored awhile, waiting for a wind, and then headed across Georgian Bay. In addition to her crew, on board were the captain's wife, Annavann Birnie, and their two small children.

By the time they approached Cabot Head on the western shore of the Bay, next evening at 5:30, the vessel was beating into a northwester under shortened sail, with the crew pumping constantly to keep the water down inside her. Then the wind shifted and began to gust, picking up planks from the deckload and driving them through the foresail, which immediately split and beat itself to pieces. As the crew fought to bring the schooner under control, the jib and staysail split in the high wind; when they jibbed her to run before the increasing gale, the main boom and gaff broke. The boom fell alongside in a tangle of rigging and canvas and lay there, threatening to batter a hole in the ship. With axes and knives the crew finally cut it away and then returned to the pumps, while the helmsman kept her running before the wind under bare masts.

In the darkness she ran past the Flowerpots and the Bear's Rump, barely clearing them, and headed down the open Bay towards Collingwood. Meanwhile Annavann Birnie and her oldest child mopped up the water that drove into the cabin and somehow kept wood dry for the stove. Annavann also managed to keep coffee boiling on the wildly swaying and pitching stove all night, handing up cups of the hot stuff to the men on the cold, wet deck. As the night went on she laced it with judicious measures of whiskey.

Next morning as dawn came the *Otonabee* swept past Craigleith; Alex Birnie and his wife could see their home there in the distance beyond the surf that pounded on the shore. The masts and rigging of their schooner were covered with ice and snow as they bore down on Collingwood. Before long it became evident that she would continue on past Collingwood and drive up somewhere on the shore beyond. Frantic efforts by the crew to get some sail on her, so that she could be manœuvred into Collingwood harbour, were fruitless; the remaining canvas was solidly frozen in ice.

The captain brought her as near the harbour entrance as he could, and dropped her big anchor as she careened along. The anchor took hold; the schooner rounded up with a jerk that almost tore her apart; and the anchor chain broke with a resounding noise. Quickly the captain ordered another anchor dropped, and then a smaller one. The crew paid out the remaining chain, then fastened on the towline and paid that out. Bow to the wind, the little schooner dropped back. The anchors held, and there she remained, diving over each oncoming wave and rising to meet the next one; just outside the safety of the harbour.

From Collingwood the little tug *Mary Ann* came out to the rescue. Annavann saw her coming. The captain's wife knew that the tug had so little power that in that storm she probably could not pull the schooner clear of Fisherman's Point, at the harbour entrance. If the schooner's anchors held, they were safe; if not, the tug could not save them. And, being a Scot and also being well aware of the facts of seagoing life, Annavann realized that if the tug did give them a tow under those circumstances there would be a tremendous claim for salvage. So she called out to her husband that if he was going to drown them, do it in deep water; she didn't want her bairns dashed to death on Fisherman's Point. Alex understood the message. He hushed his wife and turned to call to the tug captain. They didn't need the tug then, he bellowed. They'd signal when they did.

The rest of the day the anchors held and the schooner plunged through the huge waves. Annavann busied herself in the cabin, preparing the meals and singing "Weel may the keel row." By evening the wind had died, although the waves still drove past. The *Mary Ann* came out again. This was to be a routine tow into harbour, not a salvage operation. The schooner put a line aboard the tug, the tug moved forward to take the strain off the anchor cables so they could be brought in, and the line snapped. Alex Birnie passed another, bigger line to the tug; that broke also. The tug steamed away to go home. Birnie looked at his wife and nodded. "You were right, Annavann," said he.

By morning the waves had diminished greatly. Once again the tug came out from the harbour. This time the operation went smoothly, and the *Otonabee* reached safety at last.

The two-masted schooner *Nellie Sherwood* was less fortunate. She was lost in the big storm of September 14, 1882, when the steamer *Asia* perished. Just before she disappeared the *Nellie Sherwood* was seen from a mill near Cabot Head, on the Bruce Peninsula. Robert Lymburner, one of the family who owned the mill, told the story:

> Just after we sighted the schooner a terrible northwest squall swooped down. It lifted the water into the air from the sheltered shore, it drove the rain all through the mill, and it hurled the top of a long pile of slabs into the bay. We thought of the poor little schooner, and when it cleared she was nowhere to be seen.

The three-master *A. G. Morey* was also caught in that storm and her men saw the *Sherwood* go down. She was unsuccessful in trying to rescue the crew and had to run before the storm all the way to Midland.

Strandings, wrecks, and founderings were almost commonplace. Georgian Bay had the well-earned reputation of being the most dangerous part of the Lakes. Aids to navigation were few, unmarked rocks and shoals frequent, and searoom limited. The loss of a schooner was common enough to be relatively unimportant, and the event, if it was recorded at all might be only by a name on a chart. Lottie Wolf Shoal, off Hope Island, for example, commemorates the schooner *Lottie Wolf* that sank there in 1879. It was seldom that even a signboard would be erected, such as one still visible in the 1920's on Jane Mc-Leod Island near Parry Sound, saying that the schooner *Jane McLeod*, E. D. Cameron master, had been wrecked on that island November 12, 18-- (with the date half worn away).

As the mills of Georgian Bay grew in size, the most usual cargo for schooners became lumber. It went both to ports on Lakes Huron and Michigan and to Tonowanda, for shipment to New York. A vessel of 175 feet in length was able to carry about 600,000 feet of dry lumber, stowed in the hold in alternate layers, placed at right angles to each other and extending to the sides of the vessels. The lumber would also be piled ten feet high on deck, again with some layers piled crossways to keep the cargo from shifting. Sails were shortened to raise the booms above the deck load. Such a vessel in the open Lakes was an odd sight indeed. She almost seemed to be a large pile of lumber moving to its destination by means of its own spars, rigging, and sails.

By 1890 the number of sailing vessels on the Lakes had decreased, and by the beginning of the twentieth century only a few hundred schooners were left. Most of them were engaged in carrying lumber, however, and as lumber was still the major product of the Bay, the schooners continued to appear there in fairly large numbers. Then rather quickly they were gone. A few stragglers lasted into the 1920's, but by that time they were curiosities. Photographs taken about 1920 of the three main harbours of the Bay—Owen Sound, Collingwood, and Midland—show no sailing vessels at all. The era of sail, which had lasted over two hundred years on the Great Lakes, was ended.

In 1856 the first government lighthouse on Georgian Bay was erected on Bar Point, the long finger that extends south from Christian Island towards the mainland. This was a key spot in early navigation, for vessels coasting from Sturgeon Bay or Penetanguishene to Collingwood or Owen Sound normally passed between Christian Island and the mainland. The lighthouse was a sixty-foot stone tower, and a stone house for the keeper and his family was attached. In 1857, John Disturnell noted in one of his travel guides that there was a lighthouse at Collingwood; it was probably there as early as 1856. From his description it seems to have stood on the end of the breakwater, and it evidently was maintained by the town or the railway. There was some kind of light at Cove Island at the entrance to Georgian Bay in 1858; a passenger on the steamer *Rescue,* which passed Cove Island at 9:00 p.m. on July 12th of that year, noted that it was "merely a lantern on the top of the tower, visible about two miles on a clear night." In 1859 Canadian government lights were erected at Gig Point on Cove Island, Griffith Island on the approaches to Owen Sound, and Nottawasaga Island just off Collingwood. Probably the Cove Island light noted the preceding year was a makeshift used between the time the tower was constructed and the final installation of the light itself. In succeeding years other lights were built at other important points. In 1866 one was erected on Spider Island, and in 1870 lights were built on Lonely Island and on Red Rock. In 1872 a major storm swept away pier, breakwater, and breakwater lighthouse at Collingwood. They were rebuilt in 1873 and 1874, the cost being shared by the town, the railway, and the government. In 1875 a lighthouse was built on the Bustards and one on Gin Rock. Others followed in the 80's on Whiskey and Hope Islands and in the 90's on Giant's Tomb and the Western Islands.

The crew of an American sailing yacht that cruised on Georgian Bay in July of 1898 visited the lighthouse on Gereaux Island, off Byng Inlet. Judging by their description of life there, lighthouse-keeping at that time must have been a relaxing profession.

> At the house we were directed to inquire at a boathouse near at hand by a stout, barefooted Frenchwoman. Upon opening the door we found the keeper, a most picturesque old child of the sea, reclining in a wonderful home-made hammock, smoking a short-stemmed pipe, and recounting early adventures to a black-eyed grand-

son. He acknowledged our arrival with easy unconcern, and in a few words of broken English made us feel quite at home.

The man was a native of Montreal and had been a lightkeeper for thirty-five years. He showed them his sled dogs and his sled, and explained that the island was supplied by the steamer *Seguin*, which travelled between Montreal and Port Arthur. Most interesting, however, was the fact that his only clock was four hours fast and that as a result he had recently dined at 8:30 in the morning.

In the nineteenth century white settlement brought with it to Georgian Bay the start of commercial fishing. The Bay fishermen at first were mainly *voyageurs* from Penetanguishene and Indians, and the catch was for local consumption or was salted and sold to fish dealers who came around in small vessels. Fishermen from Penetang were at work in the 1830's. Some of the earliest fishermen at the northern end of the Bay and along the Bruce came from settlements on the Canadian side of Lake Huron. When the railway arrived at Collingwood in 1855, commercial fishing increased considerably, particularly on the adjoining Nottawasaga Bay. By 1857 John Disturnell could announce in one of his guidebooks, "Immense quantities of fish are taken in the waters of Nottawassaga [sic] Bay, being principally carried to the Toronto Market," and he quoted an estimate that the yearly value of the catch was £40,000.

About 1858 an energetic boatbuilder named William Watts moved to Collingwood from Toronto Island, where he had been building small skiffs for the previous four or five years, since arriving from Ireland. At Collingwood he continued to build his skiffs. They were about twenty feet long, sharp-sterned, and equipped with one or two spritsails. Soon there was a fleet of these Collingwood skiffs in use by the local fishermen. As competition grew among the fishermen they went farther and farther from home and, as a result, needed larger and larger boats. Watts' original model was soon enlarged and fitted with a long bowsprit and jib as well as the spritsails.

Other builders, located both in Collingwood and the other Bay towns, began to copy the Watts design. Watts boats were also sold for use in other towns. By the mid-60's fishing skiffs of the Collingwood type were common everywhere on the Bay.

Fishing boats were involved in much of the daily activity of the Georgian Bay settlements, at times in surprising ways. In April of 1866, as a result of the Fenian raids, the Owen Sound and Meaford companies of militia were ordered to duty at Sarnia. The company at Leith, a short distance outside Owen Sound, was not called up at that time. One pleasant Sunday, not long afterwards, the Rev. Alexander Hunter was conducting services in the Leith Presbyterian Church when he was interrupted by a messenger who entered the church, walked up the aisle, and whispered to a member of the congregation that Fenians had been sighted off Griffith Island, headed for Owen Sound. Pandemonium followed. The entire village lined up on the beach to watch seven vessels manœuvring under sail in the distance. The Leith militia company mobilized hurriedly and moved bravely to Owen Sound to defend the town. It was not until the next day they learned that the supposed Fenian vessels were actually local fishing boats holding a regatta.

From the start, most commercial fishing was done with gill nets, long nets held in the water by floats along the top and weights along the bottom. The early nets were made of linen, first obtained, according to story, by unravelling the old clothing of the fishermen's wives. The floats were boards about $2\frac{1}{2}$ feet square and the weights were stones. Then about 1860 cast lead sinkers and shaped cedar floats—"leads and corks" to the fishermen—came into use. The nets were raised and lowered over the sharp sterns of the Collingwood boats.

It seems to have been some time in the 70's when there arrived at Collingwood from the Atlantic Coast a man named Carmichael. He had the Watts shop build a 33- or 35-footer for him. She was by far the largest Collingwood fishing boat that had been turned out. He had the forward ten feet or so decked, and installed a couple of bunks and a stove below. She was rigged as a gaff ketch with a long bowsprit and unstayed masts, had a deck along each side, and a heavy wooden centreboard in place of the iron ones commonly used in the smaller boats. She proved successful; other fishermen liked her looks; and a number of similar boats were built, though none was ever much larger. The average length of a Collingwood skiff remained about thirty feet; in time, boats even smaller than that came to be rigged and decked like the larger craft. Carmichael's ideas put the finishing touches on the Collingwood boats. From his time on they remained about the same.

Competition continued. The fishermen went as far afield as they could on Georgian Bay and then moved on to Lake Huron; they sailed into Lake Michigan and, when that became too crowded, into Lake Superior. Wherever they went, they set up fishing camps where the fish were packed and shipped by steamer. Finally the fishermen moved on to Lake Winnipeg. Watts boats were shipped there from Collingwood by rail. A Collingwood skiff was also used in the surveys of James Bay, the lower part of Hudson Bay. The Collingwood fishing fleet was largest about 1885 and began to dwindle after that, but the Collingwood boat was taken to the Pacific Coast by a son of the William Watts who first built the type. Captain William Watts moved from the Lakes to the Pacific in 1888 and began to build skiffs of this model for the Fraser River salmon fisheries.

In a letter written fifty years later, the captain gave a convincing eulogy of the Collingwood boat:

> I have seen these same boats at their best and worst, running under bare poles for hours at a time, and I have seen them iced to their mast head and the sails crackling like magnetic sparks. I have seen them anchored in exposed positions and 2 men using buckets all night to keep them afloat. I have been on the bottoms and sides of them when they would not roll over entirely because the sails and spars kept them from going over entirely and lashing ourselves on in a heavy southeaster 10 miles to the west of Collingwood in November. I have seen us go to schooners anchored on Lafferty shoal in a fish boat when we could do nothing with the life boat. I was a member of the Collingwood Life Saving Crew for 10 years, and I

am going to say here and now, properly handled, there is no type of boat made in the same class. . . .

When the Collingwood boats first went into the upper Lakes, the only other craft fishing there were Indian canoes and a few Huron boats (the square-sterned boats used along the shores of Lake Huron proper). By the 70's, sharp-sterned boats were being built on the shores of Lake Michigan and Lake Superior for the American fishermen who had moved into these areas. They were less standardized in design than were the boats of Georgian Bay, yet there were more similarities than differences between the two types. The American boats were evidently a development of the Collingwood type, modified by the experience and ideas of the men who built and used them. All the double-ended fishing boats soon came to be called Mackinaw boats. The name Mackinaw had first been given to the flat-bottomed *bateaux* used near the strait and island of that name at an earlier period. Then it seems to have been applied to any small sailing craft on the upper Lakes. But as time passed, general usage gave the name specifically to the sharp-sterned boats.

The Collingwood Mackinaws were not only used in fishing, but they also were used as the nineteenth-century version of a family car or a pick-up truck by many people who lived in isolated places. They carried produce to market, brought provisions from town, and did similar errands. They had a fine reputation for seaworthiness. On one occasion, when a group of Collingwood fishermen led by the well-known Alex Clark, were refused permission to use the Sault canal, they shot the rapids instead and arrived quite safely, if somewhat battered, at the lower end.

Most Georgian Bay towns developed their own fleets of Mackinaw fishing boats. In Midland in the 1880's the two Yates brothers owned thirty-five boats and a freight tug that carried the catch from their various camps to their fish house at Midland. Because independent fishermen who owned their own boats also sold to the Yates, they handled, in a season, twenty-five to thirty-five tons of fish per week, and shipped it throughout Canada and the United States.

Most of the fishermen were Canadians from Collingwood, Meaford, Owen Sound, and the other Bay towns, but James Cleland Hamilton, a visitor to various Bay fishing camps in the 90's, also met several non-Canadians, including an old man from the Lewis Islands. The latter was in charge of some of the vats in which fish entrails were boiled down for oil.

His calling had a wonderful interest for the simple-minded old man, and he insisted on our visiting his den. Sitting in an oily scow, he took the oars, and passing out among some islands, and into a little bay enclosed with high rocks, we came to a shanty, with an iron crane over the doorway, and empty barrels about it. Landing, he ushered us into the rude laboratory. Noisesome messes stewed slowly in two iron vats, crude oil rising to the surface. The good man proudly exhibited his apparatus, crane, vats, barrels and stock on hand. He stirred up the simmering rich stuff, in which he seemed as interested and unconscious of any unpleasantness, as a painter mixing colors on his palette. Alas! our unaccustomed senses could not abide the terrible odors that arose. Waiting till his back was turned, we escaped and were soon breathing purer air on an adjacent mossy rock-top.

The oil was sold in Toronto for $10 to $12 a barrel. Much of the fish, on the other hand, was sold to agents of American companies. As the boats came in from the fishing grounds they were unloaded and the fish dressed and packed in ice in wheeled boxes, each of which contained 1200 pounds. These were put on the steam tugs, which carried them away. Trout and whitefish were the usual varieties caught, but in the autumn pickerel were worth more per pound than anything else because they could be shipped without first being dressed, and after arrival at market could be prepared by kosher butchers in the manner prescribed by Rabbinical law.

Fishing tugs were at first used to take the catch to the ports from which it was shipped to market. They were little steamers, perhaps sixty feet long, usually of the same kind as those used to tow log rafts and do other marine chores. They appeared on the scene by the late 50's, and in time came to be used in the actual raising and lowering of nets, and developed into something quite different from a regular tug-boat.

Time brought many changes to the tug. Gasoline and diesel engines replaced the bulky steam machinery. Pilot houses and cabins were enlarged, until many tugs had structures that covered their entire decks. Fishing in anything but summer weather had always been a brutal business. The men were exposed to wind and spray, and they raised cold wet nets that might freeze as they were piled on deck. Now fishermen on the tugs were sheltered, and the nets themselves would not freeze. The large turtle-back cabins were not graceful, but they worked. Fishing still was no easy job; the cold wet fish still had to be removed by hand from the cold wet gillnets as they came in; but it was not as bad as it once had been. Also, the mechanical net-pullers on many tugs did much of the heaviest work. Nets themselves changed with the passage of time. About 1900, cotton nets replaced linen. During the 1940's hollow plastic floats replaced the oiled cedar floats. And about 1950 nylon replaced cotton.

Steam tugs, mechanical net-lifters, and internal combustion engines have all increased the effectiveness of the fishermen. Nylon nets are about three times as efficient as the cotton nets. Thus over the years a given number of commercial fishermen have been able to exert more and more pressure on the existing fish population.

Statistics on Georgian Bay fish production are probably not always as complete or as accurate as they seem in cold print, and at different times the area included in the official definition of Georgian Bay has varied slightly. Nonetheless, the figures give a good general picture of what happened. In the mid-1870's the total combined yearly catch of whitefish, lake trout, and yellow pickerel was over two million pounds. From then until the 1950's it fluctuated between two and seven million, and registered six million pounds in 1953, most of it whitefish. After that it declined sharply; by 1960 the total was not quite 98 *thousand* pounds. It then rose slightly. The 1965 figure was 243,000 pounds.

What happened? The one definite thing that biologists seem able to link with the decline of the fisheries is the arrival in

Georgian Bay of the sea lamprey, a primitive animal that looks rather like an eel with a large sucking mouth, and that attaches itself to fish and feeds on their blood. The fish then often die from infection or loss of blood. The lampreys attack many species of fish, but the lake trout seems to be the most vulnerable, and has disappeared almost entirely from the Bay. Although the whitefish is more able to resist the lamprey attacks, it too has almost gone. Several years of improper water temperature and food, the lamprey, and intensive commercial fishing have combined to diminish its numbers.

Today fishery experts have developed ways of controlling lampreys. The control of commercial fisheries poses more of a problem however; experts do not always agree what controls are needed, or even that they are needed. Political factors complicate the picture. But Georgian Bay has already several areas that either are largely closed to commercial fishing or that are not suitable to it; these may contribute much to the whitefish population, which even in its present diminished number exceeds those of Lakes Ontario, Erie, Huron, or Michigan.

# The first steamers

The first Georgian Bay steamer was launched at the village of Penetanguishene in about 1832 by two local residents, Messrs. Thompson and Mitchell, and named, appropriately, the *Penetanguishene*. She ran between that port and Coldwater, and elsewhere on the Bay as opportunity called. The *Penetanguishene* carried some of the first settlers to their new holdings, and on at least one occasion landed them at an unexpected destination. Louis George Labatte, a blacksmith and former British soldier of French-Canadian descent, and his family, were involved. Some years later his son, Antoine Labatte, told the story.

> We left Penetanguishene in 1834, to go to Meaford to take up land received for Government service. We were in a bateau with our goods and provisions, being towed by the steamer *Penetanguishene*, on board of which were Captain Workman and family and Mr. Rattray and family, with their household furniture, also going to Meaford, accompanied by a Mr. Vail; Stephen Jeffrey [*sic*] in his sail-boat was also being towed. A heavy storm arose before we reached Christian Island. Our bateau smashed the back windows of the cabin of the little steamer, and one of the lines broke by which we were being towed. We were driven on Christian Island, near where the lighthouse stands. After a little time the

captain thought he would try again, and my father refused to go. We were obliged to unload the bateau, as it belonged to the steamer. We unloaded our goods and black-smith's tools into a birch canoe, while they started the second time for the Blue Mountains, but were obliged to return. We camped there about a week. Captain Beman came along with his sloop and took Captain Workman and his party to Meaford, but left Mr. Vail. My father found him one day without any food, and brought him to our camp. Antoine Lacourse, a fisherman from Pene-tanguishene, and some friends, came to take us back to Penetanguishene. We started, but the ice was so thick it took three men with sticks in the front of the bateau to break it. We got as far as Thunder Bay (Tiny), and landed at a fisherman's cabin, but twelve feet square, where we stayed for the night, with fifteen men, besides eight of our own family. We built a place to winter in, then built a log house, and lived on the bay ever since. The old house is still standing.

The *Penetanguishene* was apparently not well adapted to service on Georgian Bay, and economic conditions there were probably not yet such that a steamer could earn her way. She disappeared from the Bay and her departure seems to have gone unrecorded. Almost certainly, however, she was the same vessel on which Mrs. Anna Jameson rode in 1837 from Chatham to Detroit, over the River Thames and Lake St. Clair.

It is time, however, that I should introduce you to our party on board the little steam-boat, which is now puffing, and snorting, and gliding at no rapid rate over the blue tranquil waters of Lake St. Clair. First, then, there are the captain, and his mate or steersman, two young men of good manners and appearance; one English—the other Irish; one a military, the other a naval officer; both have land, and are near neighbours up somewhere by Lake Simcoe; but both being wearied out by three years solitary life in the bush, they have taken the steam-boat for this season on speculation, and it seems likely to answer. The boat was built to navigate the ports of Lake Huron from

Penetanguishene, to Goderich and St. Joseph's Island, but there it utterly failed. It is a wretched little boat, dirty and ill contrived. The upper deck, to which I have fled from the close hot cabin, is an open platform, with no defence or railing around it. . . .

We took in at Chatham a large cargo of the usual articles of exportation from Canada to the United States, viz. barrels of flour, sacks of grain, and emigrants proceeding to Michigan and the Illinois. . . .

By 1844 the road from Lake Simcoe north to Coldwater was extended on to Sturgeon Bay. Soon afterward a sloop was sailing regularly from Sturgeon Bay to Penetanguishene and Sydenham. By 1850 the sloop had been replaced by the little steamer *Gore*, travelling to Penetanguishene, Owen Sound, Manitoulin, Wallace Mine, St. Joseph, Bruce Mine, and Sault Ste. Marie.

The *Gore* must have prospered, for in 1853 a considerably larger steamer was put on the run from Sturgeon Bay to Sault Ste. Marie, with stops at ports on Georgian Bay and the North Channel. This was the *Kaloolah*, a sidewheeler 188 feet long. She had been launched at Buffalo the preceding year. Even so, the English traveller, William H. G. Kingston, who boarded her at Sturgeon Bay that autumn, was not reassured by her looks.

Had we been told that the vessel on board of which we were about to embark was built of pasteboard, we might almost have believed it. She appeared as if she was kept together alone by the huge arch which ran from her stem to her stern, but which in reality adds great strength to vessels of her construction.

Apparently there were labour problems even then. The captain and some of the mates and engineers had walked off the steamer a short time before Kingston arrived, and the stewardess had been dismissed. Their replacements were satisfactory, however. "A very steady, tall, gaunt, old West Highlander, with a round blue bonnet on his head, acted as master, aided by a most respectable young man, the owner's son; and

114

then we had a steward, Luis, an Italian, who was a host in himself,—a more active, intelligent, willing fellow I never met." Kingston and his wife were accommodated in the only private stateroom; the other berths were ranged along the sides of the saloon and the ladies' cabin. The steamer got under way at five a.m., reached Penetanguishene two hours later, and then proceeded westward.

On getting outside the harbour of Penetanguishene, we found that the expected gale had sprung up, and we began rolling, and pitching, and tumbling about in the most unenviable manner; the short chopping seas looking as if every instant they would break aboard of us and send our frail craft to the bottom. Not a stitch of canvas, nor a stick to set it on, had she to aid in steadying her; and I saw that if our machinery gave way, we must be driven, without the power of guiding ourselves, at the mercy of the winds and waves. As we could see the waves breaking with no little violence on the headlands and points to leeward, to contemplate the possibility of such a disaster was far from pleasant; so I said nothing about the matter, and endeavoured myself not to think of it. Had I known what a civil engineer, a fellow-passenger, afterwards told me, that the engine was high-pressure, and that it was terribly out of order, I should have been far less at my ease. One is apt to fancy a lake an ornamental and harmless bit of water, but I would a hundred-fold rather have been in a tolerably good ship in a heavy gale of wind in mid ocean than where we then floated on board the Kaloolah. All we could do was to sit in a sort of stern-gallery outside the saloon, holding on by the stanchions which supported the roof. . . .

As they passed Giant's Tomb Island and came into the open Bay, the steamer was exposed to the full sweep of the storm. "Our pitchings and numberless eccentric tumblifications had now reached a point which the ruling powers on board deemed no longer safe, and, fortunately, the Christian group of islands being near at hand, we ran for shelter under their lee, and anchored in a deep bay, on the rising shores of which grew so dense a forest of tall trees, that though the gale howled outside, scarcely a zephyr reached us."

At daylight next morning the steamer got under way again and went on to Collingwood. From there she proceeded to Sydenham, and after that headed north.

> All night long we were steering a northerly course along the Georgian Bay, rolling and pitching in the most disquieting manner. Our state-room was a sort of pocket out of the ladies' cabin, and having windows looking on the water, I could watch the dark leaden waves leaping and tumbling, and appearing every moment as if about to wash over our low deck and send us to the bottom. For a couple of hours or more, till we got under the lee of the Great Manitoulin Island, we were exposed to the full sweep of the Lake Huron. . . . The space between our cabin and the bulwarks was occupied by five or six Indians, men and women, habited in blanket-garments; and there they sat, crouching down side by side all night long, their long lank hair and dark brown features alone showing that their bodies were not bundles of bed-clothes.

The following year another English traveller, Laurence Oliphant, came through Sturgeon Bay. He described the passengers he saw embark there and the accommodations they found on the steamer:

> Towards evening the stages arrived with a large and nondescript cargo of passengers—emigrants from Europe, speculators from the States, tourists from all parts of the world, rough backwoodsmen, and mysterious characters, journeying towards the limits of civilisation, for reasons best known to themselves. All joined in the scramble for the berths which lined the saloon of the steamer. . . . To a person who has never made a voyage upon the American lakes in the steamboats which traverse them, the first effect is very singular. The whole passenger accommodation is upon deck. Sometimes there are cabins opening off the saloons; but in the boat we were in, the berths were screened off simply by curtains suspended to bars, which projected a little beyond the

116

berth, so that there was just room enough allowed for the process of dressing. Few persons, however, thought it necessary to make use of these, and the great majority of toilets, therefore, took place in the saloon.

Until the Northern Railway arrived at Collingwood in 1855, steamer activity on Georgian Bay was both local and limited. The railroad stimulated as great an expansion in shipping as in other things. Before long there were three distinct Georgian Bay steamer trades: local, into Lake Superior, and with Chicago or other United States ports. At times they overlapped; this was particularly true of the local and Lake Superior runs; but three separate trades were clearly evident. All of them continued until fairly recent times.

In 1855 the Sturgeon Bay route was abandoned. The *Kaloolah* was moved to Collingwood and was renamed the *Collingwood*, but she continued to sail north to the Sault. In July of 1857, she was chartered to carry to the head of Lake Superior a Canadian expedition sent west by the government to explore the resources of the Red River district. She thus became the first vessel to make the trip from a Georgian Bay port to the Lakehead.

In 1858 the twin-screw steamer *Rescue*, 121 feet long, inaugurated regular service from Collingwood to the head of Superior, carrying mail for the Red River district. The first mail consisted of three letters and two newspapers, and was in charge of Captain William Kennedy, an old Hudson's Bay Company man. The *Rescue*, with Captain James Dick as master, left Collingwood on this first trip at 10:30 in the morning on July 12th. After some intermediate stops, and after laying to in a fog six hours off Thunder Cape on Lake Superior, Captain Dick anchored his vessel outside the bar at Fort William at 7:00 p.m. on the 15th. The next morning at 8:00 he took her on to Grand Portage, arriving after dark, lay to off the entrance until daybreak, and entered Grand Portage Bay at 5:00 a.m. Captain Kennedy shook hands all round, landed, and with two Indian canoemen set out with the mail for the Red River settlement over the old canoe route.

In July of 1859 the sidewheel steamer *Ploughboy*, on the local run, distinguished herself by breaking the crosshead of her engine off Lonely Island, with Sir John A. Macdonald, then Premier of Upper Canada, on board, accompanied by members of his cabinet and political adherents. She anchored, in hopes that another vessel would pass and give her a tow. None appeared. A heavy sea rose. The anchors began to drag and she was carried slowly towards the rocky shore of the island. Some of her crew manned a small boat and headed for Owen Sound, seventy-five miles away, to get help. With them went Sheriff B. W. Smith of Simcoe County, host to the group of politicians.

As the *Ploughboy* drifted towards the rocky shore, the Speaker of the House was called upon to read the prayers for those in peril on the sea; in the absence of a clergyman, the men on board thought him most persuasive. By 2:30 in the morning she had drifted to within twenty-five fathoms of the island, carried by heavy waves which drove past her to crash on the rocks beyond. At that point her anchors held. The party in the small boat eventually landed somewhere on the Bruce Peninsula and reached Owen Sound by land. Luckily they found the steamer *Canadian* in the harbour. She immediately proceeded to the aid of the *Ploughboy*, arrived about midnight of the following day, and towed her to Collingwood. Most of the passengers returned to Toronto by the first train.

The paddle steamer *Algoma*, 163 feet on the keel, came to Collingwood in 1864 and entered the Lake Superior trade, calling at posts of the Hudson's Bay Company and little settlements along the Superior north shore, en route to Fort William. She immediately proved successful. In 1867 the Beatty family bought the town site of Parry Sound near their mill and timber holdings. That year they also had a steamer built on Lake Ontario and towed to Collingwood, where her machinery was installed. Parry Sound could only be reached by water and the steamer was a necessity if the lumber business and the community there were to develop. The new steamer was the *Waubuno*, a trim sidewheeler 135 feet long with a beam of only eighteen feet. She was a particularly capable-looking and neat little vessel; a long, unbroken hurricane deck and low pilot house gave her a sleek appearance. The *Waubuno*'s owners put her in the trade between Collingwood and the Sault, though, needless to say, she called at Parry Sound as well as at other intervening ports.

The steamers were involved in the life of the isolated Georgian Bay towns in much the same way autos later became involved. In 1867 William Beatty ran for election as Member of Parliament for Algoma, the large northern district embracing his town, Parry Sound. The nearest voting place was Sault Ste. Marie, three hundred miles to the northwest. Two steamers carried parties supporting the rival candidates. On the *Waubuno* were Beatty and over a hundred loyal voters; on the *Algoma* were partisans of Beatty's opponent, W. M. Simpson of Owen Sound. The *Waubuno* was delayed by engine trouble and did not arrive until after the polls were closed. Simpson won by nine votes.

In 1868 the *Chicora* arrived on the scene. She had been built in Liverpool as a blockade runner during the American Civil War, and her previous name is variously given as *B*, *Letter B*, and *Let Her B*. The last version is the most frequently quoted. In order to bring her to the Lakes she had been cut in two, so that she could pass through the canals, and had been joined together again at Buffalo. She was a lean vessel, with two high raking funnels that rose just fore and aft of her big paddle wheels, and a single raking mast just aft of her pilot house. She was 221 feet long, with a twenty-six-foot beam. When she reached Collingwood the *Let Her B* had no upper cabins and still carried tracks on her deck where her cannon had been mounted. She was fitted out to carry passengers, was put in the Lake Superior trade in 1869, and remained on that run until the end of navigation, 1875. Even after she had been modified for commercial use she was quite fast—and quite expensive to operate.

In the early 1860's the steamer *Clifton* ran between Collingwood and Owen Sound. At that time the harbour of Owen Sound was limited in capacity; the bar across the mouth of the Sydenham River effectively prevented vessels of any size from entering. The townspeople appealed to the government to dredge out the lower part of the river in order to improve harbour facilities, but they received the frustrating answer that the government would only dredge navigable streams. After pondering the apparent impasse for a short while, Captain W. H. Smith, who owned the *Clifton*, decided to do something about it. He stripped the steamer of all her gear, took off all of her cabin furniture, and even pumped the water out of her boilers. Then Captain Smith, standing on the hurricane deck, directed several men in one of the ship's boats to carry her anchors across the bar and drop them a safe distance beyond. When they splashed into the river he gave another order, and the anchor cables were heaved in. The lightened vessel pulled herself slowly across the bar into the river. He repeated the performance several times until finally she reached a landing a little way upstream. Thus he demonstrated that the river was navigable; in due course government dredging operations began there.

The *Clifton* was retired at the end of the 1866 season, and her machinery was put in the new *Frances Smith*, a 182-foot paddle steamer built in Owen Sound, the first of any size to be launched on Georgian Bay. She was also the last to sail regularly between Owen Sound and Collingwood; when a railway finally came to Owen Sound in 1873 she was put in the Lake Superior trade.

The Northern Railway itself chartered from United States owners five handsome big sidewheelers early in 1855 and at the opening of navigation four of them, the *Lady Elgin, Keystone State, Queen City*, and *Niagara*, began to run from Collingwood to Chicago and the fifth, the *Louisiana*, from Collingwood to Green Bay, Wisconsin. They were some of the finest vessels of their day, ranging from 223 to 278 feet in length; each had saloons the length of the upper deck and stateroom accommodations for nearly 300 passengers.

These were the vessels John Disturnell spoke of in his description of Collingwood: "Great numbers of travellers and emigrants are at this point transferred to magnificent steamers, bound for Mackinac, Green Bay, Chicago, and the Great West. . . ." They carried sizable cargoes as well as passengers, including the household effects of the many Scandinavian

120

emigrants passing through Collingwood *en route* to the country west of Lake Michigan.

On September 22, 1856, the 255-foot *Niagara*, fully laden with merchandise, carrying 200 deck passengers and 100 cabin passengers, left Collingwood and started north and west, calling at Mackinac Island, Two Rivers, and Sheboygan. She departed Sheboygan about 2:00 in the afternoon on September 24th; about 4:00 it was discovered she was on fire.

The flames spread outward from the engine room. A passenger heard the helmsman call for help. He joined him in the pilot house and they managed to head the burning vessel towards shore, two or three miles away, but the engines stopped five minutes later. Passengers rushed to the boats, took possession of them, and prevented the crew from lowering them properly. The mate got the large boat at the stern lowered to the level of the main deck and collected in it a number of passengers, mainly women. Then a large man burst from the cabin and leaped in. His weight snapped the fall at one end of the boat and that end dropped, spilling out the people; the full weight of the boat then snapped the rope at the other end and it plunged into the water, turning bottom up. About thirty other passengers and crew members got off on planks from the forward end of the steamer; she drifted away from them and most of them were later picked up by rescue craft. Ropes were let down from the stern of the *Niagara* down which people slid and hung in clusters until the ropes burned off.

The steamer *Traveller* was about to take on wood at a landing not far away. Captain Sweeney, her master, at once headed her for the *Niagara*, using anything loose on board as fuel in place of the wood he had not had time to load. He was able to pick up twenty-five or thirty survivors and to take the burning hulk in tow, but the line soon burned through and what was left of the *Niagara* sank about two miles from shore. Other vessels came to the scene and picked up survivors. No one seems to have known exactly how many people were on board at the time of the fire; there were conflicting reports as to the numbers that had gone ashore at the various places she had called. No one seems to have known exactly how many were saved. Informed estimates of the number who died range as high as 150. This was the first marine disaster to affect Collingwood. The people of the small port knew the steamer well, and Collingwood men were members of her crew.

Because of this disaster, and a major depression and financial panic in 1857, steamer service from Collingwood to the United States was discontinued. The next year four other ships, the *Montgomery, Ontonogon, Hunter*, and *Evergreen City*, were placed on the same run. These were a new kind of vessel. Previously the line was made up of big sidewheelers, but these were more compact propellers, ranging in length from 175 to 204 feet. The Northern Railway was back in the steamer business, but evidently it was trying to make the operation look as different as possible from the one that had included the *Niagara*.

The American Civil War brought much friction between the United States and Canada. Towards the end of the war the Canadian Government seized the propellor *Georgian* at Collingwood, where she was being fitted out as a Confederate privateer. After the war there were a number of armed raids made upon Canada from the United States by Fenians, members of an Irish patriotic group made up largely of former Union Army soldiers. In 1869, when Canada took over the western territories of the Hudson's Bay Company, the residents of the Red River Colony rose in rebellion and executed a young Canadian who opposed them. Several agents of the United States, both official and unofficial, stepped in to help the rebels.

Canada promptly made the area a new province, Manitoba, but it also sent a military expedition of about a brigade to hold it. The force, under Colonel G. J. Wolseley, a brilliant 37-year-old British officer (later Commander-in-Chief of the British Army), embarked through Collingwood at the beginning of navigation in 1870. Meanwhile the United States decided to close the Sault Ste. Marie Canal, through which the expedition was to pass, to all Canadian vessels. The *Algoma*, carrying a group of workmen and *voyageurs* who were to assist the expedition, slipped through, but shortly afterward the *Chicora*, with a similar group, was turned back by the American authorities.

After considerable diplomatic manœuvring, the United States agreed that Canadian ships could again pass through the canal, but military supplies and soldiers could not. They had to be unloaded, taken over the portage road on the Canadian side, and then put back on the steamer at the Lake Superior end. This was done; the expedition continued; and when it finally arrived at the Red River Colony the rebellion collapsed.

Georgian Bay vessels were deeply involved in moving the expedition. The *Algoma* and *Chicora*, which made regularly scheduled commercial runs from Collingwood to the Lakehead, provided the main line of communications; while the *Frances Smith* and *Waubuno* made trips from Collingwood to the Sault and American vessels were hired to carry some of the men and cargoes from that point on. In order to guard Collingwood, the Sault, and the vessels moving between them from threatened Fenian attacks, the Canadian Government brought to the Bay two small gunboats, the *Rescue* and the *Prince Alfred*, which patrolled back and forth that summer.

Meanwhile Canadians were looking westward. When Manitoba was created a province in 1870, she had as yet no rail connection with the older parts of Canada, and the steamer trade from Georgian Bay to the Lakehead flourished. There was competition however; in 1871 the Northwest Navigation Company began sending vessels out of Sarnia on Lake Huron.

The steamers carried freight, mail, and passengers. The Lake Superior voyage during the summer months also attracted many travellers bent on pleasure. One account of a trip from Collingwood to Lake Superior in July of 1871 includes the remark, "At half past four p.m. the 'Chicora' leaves the wharf and we are out on the bay, some sixty-five of us in all, at least fifty of whom are taking the round trip." John Disturnell, in a travel guide published at Philadelphia in 1874, says, "Of all the approaches to Lake Superior from the Atlantic Seaboard, or from Montreal and Quebec, nothing exceeds the *Collingwood Route* for grand and varied Lake, Island, and River Scenery. . . ." Among the back pages of Disturnell's book is a full-page advertisement for the Lake Superior Royal Mail Line, "In connection with the Northern Railway of Canada," which states, "This line embraces *Three*

*Magnificent, First-Class, Upper Cabin*, Side-Wheel Steamers, viz:—CHICORA, CUMBERLAND, AND FRANCES SMITH." According to the advertisement they left Collingwood every Tuesday and Friday for a long list of Georgian Bay and Lake Superior ports. In heavy type, half way down the page, is an offering of excursion rates during the summer months.

In November 1872 the 120-foot steamer *Mary Ward* was brought to Georgian Bay to be used in the Lake Superior trade the following year. She entered the Bay, called at Owen Sound on Sunday the 24th, and proceeded towards Collingwood, which was to be her home port. At 9:00 p.m. on a clear, warm night off Craigleith she ran on a shoal that is now called the Mary Ward Shoal. She was far off her proper course, and how this happened has never been well explained. The common story of the day that she picked up the light of a Craigleith tavern and confused it with the lighthouse is scarcely believable, unless it was a sly way of saying that someone aboard was more interested in alcohol than in piloting.

The warm, calm night was a typical weather-breeder for that season, but the captain let everyone settle down, apparently thinking she could be pulled off the next day. Only two men went ashore, Frank Moberly, a passenger, one of the well-known Georgian Bay family, and with him one of the vessel's owners. They set out by land for Collingwood to get help.

A passenger described what happened next:

> I was anxious and did not go to my cabin, although all the rest retired for the night. I sat up on deck. Shortly after midnight the wind suddenly shifted and heavy, black, swiftly moving clouds arose over the mountain and the stars soon disappeared. There was an ominous moaning in the rigging, the import of which I knew too well. There was an uncanny stillness. I shall never, as long as I live, forget the weird feeling of alarm and terror which came over me, nor shall I ever wholly forgive myself for not acting on the impulse I had to arouse everyone and tell them that a storm was about to break and

that we better get to land while there was time. But I had no authority and being young I was reluctant to exhibit signs of fear. After a little time I did suggest to the watchman that he call the Captain. This he did and the Captain realized the danger at once and began blowing the *Mary Ward*'s whistle again frantically and calling all hands on deck. The storm increased in fury suddenly and by dawn huge breakers were sweeping over the stern. Had she not been well built she would have gone to pieces in a very short time but she held together despite the tremendous strain and pounding. In a few hours we were all hanging on for dear life and most of us had become reconciled to our fate. We were all soaking wet and cold. A few of the passengers, becoming desperate, foolishly launched a life boat in an endeavor to make land. Eight men got into it but they were only a few yards from the steamer when they were overturned and all were drowned. The rest of us clung to the stranded steamer and were rescued later in the day by some fishing boats.

Moberly and his companion reached Collingwood about seven in the morning. They alerted the tug *Mary Ann*, owned by the Moberlys, but by the time she got up steam the seas were so big that she could not venture out into them. Shortly after the fishing boats took off the remaining people in the late afternoon, the *Mary Ward* went to pieces.

Along with the increase in westward trade, the local Bay trade was also developing. Captain Peter M. Campbell, who had been master of the *Waubuno* for several years, left the employ of the Beattys, her owners, and formed a syndicate of a few men to bring another steamer into the trade. They called their organization the Georgian Bay Navigation Company. It bought a recently built American vessel, renamed her *Northern Belle*, and in 1876 put her in service on the Bay, visiting ports from Collingwood to Sault Ste. Marie in competition with the *Waubuno*.

Captain Campbell, one of the many Scottish-Canadians who became Lake captains, was one of the best known. He usually was called Black Pete because of his black hair and the fierce black whiskers that ringed his face. He shaved his upper lip so that his features appeared clean-shaven within the circling growth of hair. Black Pete Campbell was a dashing character, always ready to race a competing steamer, always full of flair. He would leave port during a storm, set his course, and then go calmly to his bunk. He was steady and resourceful in a tight place, however, as he was to demonstrate fully some years later when the *Manitoulin*, which he was then commanding, burned near Manitowaning.

The members of the new company and the Beattys soon began negotiations that ended in the amalgamation of the two concerns. In this way the Beatty family obtained an interest in the Georgian Bay Navigation Company, and the company operated both steamers. But some competition still existed on the Bay. Byng Inlet lumber interests built their own hundred-footer, the *Maganettawan*, in 1877 and ran her over essentially the same route.

The autumn of 1879 saw a series of November storms on the Lakes. The *Waubuno*, enroute to Parry Sound, had been delayed in Collingwood. Her cargo was overdue on the North Shore, and her crew and passengers were beginning to grumble. Among those on board were a young doctor and his new bride, starting north to set up a practice. Next morning at breakfast the young wife told of a dream that the *Waubuno* had been wrecked and all on board drowned; her husband scoffed, but she remained worried. The story was passed around the boat and then to some people in town. Perhaps the passengers and crew did whisper that Captain George Burkett actually believed in this foolishness and that that was why he kept the *Waubuno* in port; perhaps the captain knew that they were whispering. In any event, the wind abated at four and the captain suddenly took her out into the night, leaving behind in Collingwood, without warning, a number of intended passengers.

She never arrived at Parry Sound. The rival steamer *Maganettawan* came in the following Monday and her crew asked about the other vessel, but no one worried greatly; she undoubtedly had taken refuge somewhere along the way. Possibly she was aground. The *Mittie Grew*, a lumber tug, went down the South Channel to find out. Just below Copperhead she discovered wreckage all along the shore. There was much evidence that the *Waubuno* had been wrecked, but no bodies were found—then or ever afterward.

Loggers who had been working near Moon River on the 22nd later reported that during a heavy snow storm, near noon, they had heard a ship whistling as though she were in distress. The next March an Indian found the *Waubuno* hull upside down, on the shore of what now is called Wreck Island.

The *Waubuno*'s exact fate was long one of the great mysteries of Georgian Bay. In recent years, however, skin divers have investigated the waters in which she perished and as a result a great deal is now known, or can be deduced, about her fate. Evidently she attempted to enter her usual approach to Parry Sound, the narrow Waubuno Channel, was blinded by the snow storm, turned back, and tried to slip through the gap at Copperhead. It probably was then that she was heard whistling. Captain Burkett dropped his anchors, but the waves threw the vessel about so that the upper works began to break off, and the anchors tore loose and let her slide down-wind to a shoal where the breakers apparently picked her up, turned her on her side, and smashed her down so hard that the main engine was dashed through the side of the hull, and the hull split in two lengthwise. The upper works, carrying the bodies of all twenty-four persons on board, must have drifted off down-wind to sink in deep water.

# The fleets come—and go

The owners of the foundered *Waubuno* soon became targets of damage suits brought by the families of those lost with her. A special court was convened to hear them all, but in the end all were dismissed for lack of evidence. The company meanwhile was reorganized. More shareholders were brought in; the name was changed to Great Northern Transit Company; and in 1880 the 147-foot propeller *Manitoulin*, which had just been built at Owen Sound, was purchased and put in service to replace the *Waubuno*.

The company also brought a vessel from Lake Ontario to Georgian Bay and renamed her the *Emerald*. The Great Northern was forming a fleet. They already had the *Northern Belle* and in 1878 (as the Georgian Bay Navigation Company) had purchased a vessel in the United States, renaming her the *Northern Queen*. In 1880 they acquired the rebuilt *Simcoe* and put her in the Collingwood-Chicago trade until she sank, later that year.

The *Manitoulin* followed a regular schedule throughout 1880 and 1881, with Captain Peter M. Campbell as master. On May 17, 1882, she sailed from Collingwood. Next day at noon she was proceeding quietly about four miles from the town of Manitowaning; the captain and most of the passengers were dining. Someone called "Fire!" Captain Campbell went quickly below, found the engine room in flames, and returned to the dining room to order that all passengers don life preservers. He then hurried to the bridge, where he headed the steamer for the shore—about a mile away—at full speed. In the meantime the lifeboats were swung out and a deckhand was busy throwing over the side 500 pounds of blasting powder consigned to the Canadian Pacific Railway construction crews in the north.

Chief Engineer Lockerbie went down into the burning engine room, from which his assistants had fled, and held open the throttle at maximum speed. Some of those on board ignored the captain's instructions and jumped overboard in panic; as a result eleven were lost. Six minutes after she changed course the flaming *Manitoulin* grounded on the beach, in water so shallow that all aboard could wade ashore. The pilot house was burning over the heads of First Mate Playter and Captain Campbell. They were the last to leave the vessel; Black Pete Campbell went over the side carrying a child in his arms.

The Great Northern Transit Company, never put down by a loss, decided to charter another steamer to continue the schedule of the burned *Manitoulin*. It turned to the Northwest Navigation Company of Sarnia, owned by the Beatty family and familiarly known as the Beatty Line, and from it obtained the wooden propeller *Asia*, then nine years old. During the early part of that season she had made several trips carrying cargo for the Canadian Pacific Railway construction crews working along the Lake Superior north shore.

The *Asia* was only 136 feet long on the keel. She was a canaller, built to pass through the Welland Canal of those days, which could take nothing longer than 140 feet. She was therefore designed to carry as much as possible in her short length. Immediately above her hull, which had relatively low freeboard, rose the straight wooden sides enclosing her main deck. The upper deck was surrounded by an open railing, and cabins ran most of its length. The small octagonal pilot house with a pointed roof stood on top of the forward end of the long cabin structure. Such a vessel presented rather a top-heavy appearance, but her superstructure was comparatively light and with cargo in her hold she could stand up well enough.

The *Asia*, with Captain Savage as master, steamed out of Collingwood harbour on September 13, 1882, called at Owen Sound, and left there about 1:00 a.m. on the 14th. The autumn movement to the North Shore lumber camps had begun. The *Asia* carried provisions, teams of horses, equipment, and loggers. She was heavily laden and much of the cargo was on deck, some even on the hurricane deck, to avoid the extra handling necessary to stow it in the hold and then unload it from there. She had well over a hundred people on board. The exact number does not seem to have been recorded, but it was far more than her staterooms could accommodate. They slept on the decks and on the rugs in the public cabins.

During the night, a south-east gale rose. About seven in the morning the *Asia* turned to head towards the lumber centre of French River, a port of call on that trip. She then presented her side to the wind and waves, and trouble began. When it was all over there were only two survivors, a boy and a girl, both in their teens. The boy, Dunk Tinkiss, who was travelling with his uncle, gave this description of what happened:

> At about 7:30 a.m. we all arose and had breakfast, after which we walked about. The wind at this time was blowing a stiff gale, but no one apprehended any danger whatever. As a large number felt rather sea-sick the majority returned to their berths, my uncle and myself among the rest. When I arose in the morning I was under the impression that the state-rooms were all full, as a large number of persons were on sofas and on the cabin floor. At eleven o'clock my uncle was awakened by the rolling of the ship and springing out shouted to me, "Dunk, jump up, the boat is doomed!" The expression on his face was alone sufficient to convince me that it was only too true, and throwing on my coat we both rushed on deck. The sight that met my eyes was a fearful one and one that I shall never forget. The storm was raging, the wind blowing a perfect hurricane and the waves appeared to be rolling mountains high. This was not all,

for nearly all the passengers by this time had come on deck and the scene which followed was a most heart-rending one and entirely beyond description. Until my dying day I shall never forget the cries and shrieks, a majority being on their knees, crying for mercy and deliverance, and all realizing that they were face to face with death. I at once went to a state-room and put on a life-preserver, and again returned to the deck. Those not on their knees rushed frantically about, thus adding to the general confusion. I did not see the captain or crew, and in fact I do not think they could have been of any service what ever; but I heard a single order to throw the cargo overboard. Being on the upper deck, I could not see what was going on below, but from the noise which I heard I am under the impression that the order was obeyed. No attempt was made to lower the ship's boats, as they would at once have been dashed to pieces, so for a long half-hour we stood there face to face with death, and not knowing at what instant we would be hurled into eternity. The steamer had got into the trough of the sea, and though her engines worked hard the vessel refused to obey her helm. Wave after wave swept over us, each of which threatened to engulf us, until one larger than the rest struck us, and the boat careened over. As soon as we felt her going we all sprang on the hurricane deck, in order to afford us another half minute's respite. I cannot attempt to describe the feelings of those people when they felt the boat sinking under their feet without the slightest hope of safety. You must be in the same position to realize it. It was but the work of a moment, for as she went over the water rushed over amid the heart-rending cries of those poor helpless creatures. Her stern went foremost, and she was swallowed up by the angry waves. For a brief period the upper deck and the steamer's boats floated, and noticing one I called to my uncle to follow me, and made a rush for it. He did not come, and that was the last I saw of him. I got into this one, but it was overloaded, and immediately turned over, and as a number of persons were clinging to my life-preserver, threatening to draw

131

me under I disengaged it and struck out for another boat which I saw. In it there were only eighteen persons, including the captain, the mate, the purser, and fifteen others. Thinking it my last hope I called to Mr. McDougall, the purser, to give me his hand. He did so, but exclaimed, "Oh, I don't think it of any use." As soon as I got in I looked towards the wreck, where nothing was to be seen but a struggling mass of humanity, who were clinging to pieces of timber and other wreckage to prolong their lives even for a few seconds. I saw a third boat, but it filled with water and sank. I hope I shall never see such a sight again, and as our boat drifted out of sight I felt some relief at having such misery shut out from view.

The lifeboat had water-tight compartments and would not sink, even though it turned over, again and again, as waves struck it. Tinkiss was at one end of it; the girl, Christine Morrison, was at the other. They soon remained in the water, holding on to the ends of the boat as it turned over. As it turned it struck and injured many of the men, who then were swept away. Finally the weather became a little calmer and the boat floated right side up, but it was full of water. There were no oars—only one useless paddle. In addition to the two young people, five others remained. One by one they died. The last was Captain Savage.

Towards morning the captain appeared to drop asleep, and going towards him, I shook him, asking him to wake up. He merely answered "Yes" and on repeating it said he would be up in a minute. A huge wave then struck me from him and when I returned he was dead.

The youthful vitality of the two survivors apparently kept them going. Tinkiss said that it never occurred to him that he might die and the girl seemed to feel the same way. At day break the boat drifted ashore. Miss Morrison was exhausted, but Tinkiss was able to remove the bodies from the boat and then try to paddle it towards a derrick—which at first they mistook for a lighthouse—a few miles away. By dark they had only gone half a mile. They slept on the beach that night. Next morning they reached the derrick. Nobody was there, but then an Indian passed in a boat and Tinkiss hailed him. He gave them some food, their first in two and a half days, and in return for Tinkiss' gold watch took them to Parry Sound. The impact of their story on the people there can be imagined. They were treated with the utmost kindness and it was not long before the young survivors recovered from their experience. Tinkiss lived until 1910 and Miss Morrison, who later became Mrs. Albert Fleming, until 1937.

In 1878 the New England Transportation Company was formed to run steamers between Chicago and Collingwood. The name was probably chosen to emphasize the ease of shipment from Chicago to the U.S. east coast, using water to Collingwood and rails beyond. The moving spirit of the company was Captain J. B. Fairgrieve of Hamilton. He put four steamers on the route in 1879. All were typical Welland-Canal-type vessels, in appearance much like the *Asia*, and all were about the same size, approximately 140 feet long. The line prospered so that in 1881 it also chartered the 156-foot single screw *Northern Queen* from the Great Northern Transit Company.

During bad weather that same autumn, the company lost the *Columbia* and two other steamers, but it managed to charter several United States vessels and continued to carry many passengers and much freight.

In 1882 Henry Beatty became General Manager of the marine operations of the Canadian Pacific Railway, which had decided to establish its own steamer line. He had been one of the owners of the Northwest Transportation Company—the Beatty Line—of Sarnia, and thus was one of the relatively few men who knew how to run a major shipping line on the Upper Lakes. At first the C.P.R. intended its steamers to go from Algoma Mills, on the North Shore, to Port Arthur at the Lakehead. Facilities at Algoma Mills could not be readily provided, however. As a result of Beatty's recommendations, the Board of Governors of the C.P.R. instead took up the lease on the Toronto, Grey and Bruce Railway, which ran into Owen Sound, making that port the base of their new steamship line.

Immediately there was a great scrambling by citizens of Owen Sound to make their harbour ready. It had to be dredged to accommodate the big ships. A group of Owen Sound men learned that two dredges, four scows, and one tug were to be sold in Collingwood the next Monday. The town baker and confectioner, James McLaughlan, was deputized to go to Collingwood to buy a dredge and some of the other equipment. On Monday morning he dropped off the train before it reached the Collingwood station, went to the docks, and bought one dredge, two scows, and a tug. It then occurred to him that when the people of Collingwood learned what was up they could use the other dredge to get their harbour deepened first. He immediately purchased it and the remaining two scows. Although he did not have enough money to make the required ten percent deposit on everything he now had bought, he found someone who was willing to lend him what he needed. After the ice went out that spring, dredging began within two weeks at Owen Sound harbour.

The Canadian Pacific Line running out of Owen Sound cut deeply into the Lake Superior traffic from Collingwood. The companies at Collingwood still ran some vessels into Superior, but they were not as well adapted to the service as those of the C.P.R. The Canadian Pacific Line continued to profit and grow.

In the local trade, in 1882, the Great Northern Transit Company rebuilt the burned *Manitoulin*, giving her the new name *Atlantic*. In 1883 they discarded the *Emerald* and launched the new *Pacific* at the Simpson yard at Owen Sound.

The company fixed its own rates without competition and the North Shore inhabitants paid what was set. Their dissatisfaction grew. Finally, in 1890, a group of lumbermen formed the North Shore Navigation Company, Ltd. Among the shareholders was A. M. Dodge of New York, who had sizable interests on the North Shore. Most of the other men lived at various points on Georgian Bay. They built the *City of Midland* and launched her at Owen Sound in 1890. She was a wooden propeller, 176 feet long, and was painted black, as their later vessels, in contrast to the white paint of the Great

Northern steamers. The two companies quickly became known as the Black Line and the White. Rates were slashed. Whenever two steamers of the competing lines found themselves on the same run at the same time, a race was inevitable. In 1892 a Manitoulin Island newspaper reported:

> Capt. Pete Campbell of the *Pacific* came in Wednesday with three niggers and a Sheguiandah cheese on the safety valve and the keel carefully greased to prevent friction. The story they brought was that they had beat the *City of Midland* by five minutes and 37.12076 seconds between Collingwood and Owen Sound. You could see the Cap's smile half way to Strawberry shining like the church steeple and his chin whisker was sticking out at an angle of 90 degrees with excitement, while his hat was tied on with a stout piece of hawser, and in each boot was a flat iron to keep him from blowing off the hurricane deck. Few and short were the words he said and his story was briefer than a guinea pig's tail. Then the *Pacific* steamed out, making 22 knots and smoking at every seam. Two hours after the *City of Midland* hove in sight, throwing the foam from her bow six feet into the air and twenty feet on each side of her like great white wings, belching forth rolling masses of smoke and looking thoroughly business-like in her neat black coat. Her story was also brief, and Capt. Bassett once more started on the trail of the *Pacific* with blood in his eye. All the paint was burnt off her smokestack.

The lumbermen must have been thoroughly angry with the Great Northern, for they set out not merely to force down its rates, but to kill it. In 1892 they took over the Meaford Transportation Company's 130-foot *Favourite*, next year absorbing the company and renaming the vessel *City of Parry Sound*. They also absorbed the Penetanguishene, Midland, and Parry Sound run of the Georgian Bay and Muskoka Navigation Company, which operated the *Manitou*. In 1893 they built the *City of Collingwood*, a wooden propeller 213 feet long, at Owen Sound. In 1895 they replaced the *Manitou* with a new 150-foot sidewheeler, *City of Toronto*. They brought a small vessel from Lake Ontario, renamed her *City of London*, and put her on the Spanish River run. Their service now covered the entire North Shore and North Channel and extended into Lake Superior. The owners of the White Line, in response to this attack, added to their existing fleet, launching the *Majestic*, a wooden steamer 209 feet long, at Collingwood in 1895, and the 190-foot *Germanic*, the last wooden ship built there, in 1899.

That year the North Shore Navigation Company finally bought out the Great Northern Transit Company and formed the Northern Navigation Company of Ontario, Ltd. They also absorbed the Northwest Transportation Company—the Beatty Line—which then was running two large wooden steamers between Sarnia, on Lake Huron, and the head of Lake Superior. The Beatty Line became the Lake Superior Division, and the combined Black and White Lines became the Georgian Bay Division. The headquarters of the entire organization remained at Collingwood. The last scheduled trip to the Lakehead from Collingwood was made by the *City of Collingwood* in 1900. In 1902 the *Huronic*, a steel ship 308 feet long, was launched at Collingwood for the Lake Superior Division. She was the first steel ship built there. Her launching was an omen: in the future the best products of the Collingwood shipyards would go into service elsewhere.

The Collingwood steamers had been devoted to the local trade on Georgian Bay and to some degree along the northern shore of Lake Superior. They were designed for this purpose. But the local trade was dwindling. Railways were being extended and the lumber industry, long a mainstay of local steamers, was passing.

H. H. Gildersleeve, member of a well-known family of shipowners, a man experienced in Lake Ontario shipping, was appointed manager of the Northern Navigation Company in 1904. He was a firm and outspoken man, and when he saw that most of the company business was at Sarnia, he began to press for the transfer there of the head office. Naturally the Collingwood city fathers disagreed strongly. Gildersleeve was not well liked in Collingwood. On Jaunary 1, 1909, the Grand Trunk and Grand Trunk Pacific Railways commenced delivering to

136

the Lake Superior Division at Sarnia their entire passenger and freight traffic to Port Arthur, Fort William, and Duluth. In 1910 Gildersleeve prevailed, and the company moved to Sarnia, on Lake Huron. The local trade on Georgian Bay disappeared gradually. Collingwood as a shipping centre was through.

Although the headquarters of the Northern Navigation Company had moved to Sarnia, Georgian Bay men continued to sail on steamers of the line. One of them who was particularly hard-headed is responsible for the funnel colours worn today by vessels of the mammoth Canada Steamship Lines. In 1913 the Northern was merged with the Richelieu and Ontario Navigation Company to form C.S.L. That spring two Georgian Bay sailors went to Sarnia to take over the *Huronic*; Andy Campbell, son of the legendary Black Pete, as master, and Oscar Wing, a Parry Sound man, as mate. Northern Navigation vessels had had the funnel colours of the old Beatty Line, orange-red with a white band and black top. Now, however, the new company was to have a new combination, a dull red and black. When the two men arrived at Sarnia they discovered that all of the fleet except their boat had already had their stacks repainted in the new colours. The *Huronic* still had the old ones, and although the paint was a season old the colours were still a good deal brighter and to their eyes a good deal handsomer than the new.

As mate, Oscar Wing had charge of repainting the stack. Captain Campbell, a day or so later, woke up to the fact that his new command now had the brightest, shiniest, orange-red, white, and black funnel possible. He walked over to his mate and again showed him the orders from the Montreal office stating that they were to use dull red and black. Oscar was not easily persuaded. "Leave her that way over the weekend, anyway," he said. "We owe it to the people of Sarnia."

The captain agreed, but when the local company agent saw what had happened he objected violently. After he calmed down a bit, however, he decided that the stack of the *Huronic* really looked considerably better than the others. He sent off a telegram to Montreal. Before long, word came back that the Northern Navigation Division of C.S.L. would use the old colours. Oscar Wing had won a partial victory. It was not complete until 1921, however, after he himself had been a captain for some time; that year Canada Steamship Lines adopted orange-red, white, and black for all of their vessels. They still use those colours today.

After the last trip of the *City of Collingwood* in 1900, Owen Sound was the only Bay port from which vessels sailed on a regular schedule to the head of the Lakes. The C.P.R. steamers won fame for their luxury and efficiency. Bernard McEvoy, a newspaperman who rode on the *Athabasca* in 1902, wrote:

> The deft and polite waiters are in the whitest of white jackets. The woodwork walls, perforated with innumerable doors with bright brass handles that open into the state-rooms, are painted white. The elegantly carved rafters that support the roof and form a pleasant vista are white. Everything is spic and span, and the flowers on the tables give a note of colour that is delightful. One-half of the long saloon is dining-room, and the other half— well, just saloon—thickly carpeted with a crimson carpet, into which the foot slips noiselessly, besprinkled with crimson velvet sofas and easy chairs. A piano is there, too, on which some kind amateur is sure to perform, probably pounding out harmonies that are as mechanically regular as the thud of the engine. . . .

Owen Sound however had its problems. The railroad to the town from Toronto travelled over difficult terrain, so difficult that it was first constructed as a narrow gauge line. It long since had been widened to standard gauge, but the steep grades remained. After dealing with this situation for many years, the C.P.R. finally decided to establish its own harbour at a place more easily accessible by rail. Just east of Midland they constructed a new port, with docks, freight sheds, and grain elevators—Port McNicoll. On May 1, 1912, the Canadian Pacific fleet, after operating out of Owen Sound for twenty-seven years, left that city for the last time. As the citizens watched, the five vessels sailed at five-minute intervals, beginning at 8:00 a.m. Thereafter only the *Manitoba*—the one ship of the fleet that had been built at Owen Sound—called there as she went to and from Lake Superior.

In 1897 Parry Sound finally got its rail connection with the outside world and in 1899 the railway became part of the Canada-Atlantic Railway, which then stretched from Portland, Maine to Depot Harbour, five miles from Parry Sound. John Randolph Booth, the Ottawa lumber giant, had turned to railroading with vigour and imagination. This was his line.

Depot Harbour is an excellent natural haven, and Lake vessels were soon running between it and the ports of Chicago and Milwaukee. All of them were freighters and most were package freighters; the passenger business was fading, but merchandise was still moving by water. Imports from Europe were delivered quickly to the American Midwest via Georgian Bay, and exports to Europe flowed back the same way. Most of the Chicago and Milwaukee trade was handled by vessels of the Canada-Atlantic Transit Company, a subsidiary of the railway. Vessels of other owners came also to Depot Harbour; most of them big bulk carriers bringing grain from the head of Lake Superior.

The Canada-Atlantic Railway in time was sold to the Grand Trunk, and later that became part of the Canadian National Railway, but the shipping line retained its original name until it stopped operations during World War II. Among its earliest vessels were the *Arthur Orr, George N. Orr, Scranton*, and *Ottawa*. It was the *Ottawa* which foundered on Lake Superior in November 1909, coming from Port Arthur to Depot Harbour with a full load of grain and flour. Her crew, who had taken to a lifeboat, saw her roll violently; something fell on the whistle cord; and she dove under the surface with her whistle blowing.

After 1901, when a short rail line was run directly into town from a junction with the Canada-Atlantic two miles to the east, Parry Sound itself developed a busy harbour. Vessels such as the *Turret Cape, Turret Crown*, and *Turret Court* sailed regularly from there into Lake Superior.

At Midland lived a clever man who, in 1880, at the age of 19, had come out with his parents from Scotland; who had come to Midland in 1883; and who had ridden to some fortune and local fame on the Georgian Bay lumber boom. He was James Playfair. Shortly before the turn of the century he began to dabble in Lake shipping, concentrating on bulk freighters; he bought his first vessel in 1896, had her rebuilt and renamed *Saint Andrew*, and put her in the developing grain trade from Port Arthur to the lower Lakes. Legend says that she earned her full cost the first year. She was wrecked on Lake Superior in 1900. In 1901 Playfair and a partner, D. L. White, Jr., incorporated the Midland Navigation Company and had the steel canaller *Midland Queen* built that year in Scotland. In 1903 they had the 366-foot *Midland King* built at Collingwood and in 1907 the 486-foot *Midland Prince* at the same yard. This company was involved in a series of mergers, and in 1912 the partners started building up two other fleets, the Great Lakes Transportation Company and the Glen Line. The first consisted of large Upper Lake freighters; the second of canallers. (By this time the canals took vessels up to 260 feet long, and canallers were merely small lake freighters within those dimensions.)

James Playfair had heavy eyebrows, a dark, neatly trimmed small beard, and flowing moustache. He was usually casual about his dress—photographs show him with his hat on the back of his head or the knot of his necktie at an angle—but on state occasions, as when he was entertaining on his yacht, the *Pathfinder*, or the later and larger *Venetia*, he dressed well and for the event. He was rather a stern host. On the *Venetia* his guests were awakened, summoned to meals, and sent to bed with bugle calls played by the ship's trumpeter. One wonders whether he enforced this custom during the cruise on which he entertained the Duke of Devonshire, then Governor-General of Canada.

Playfair played well the part of Merchant Prince. His home, "Edgehill," above Midland harbour, was a large wooden structure with turrets and a spacious veranda from which he could look down, first on his lumber mill and later on his shipyard. In the early days Mrs. Playfair and he rode about town in a handsome victoria with a coachman on the box driving a matched pair. Later they rode in Packard limousines and the coachman became a chauffeur. The Playfairs were also vigorous members of the Presbyterian church in Midland. When a new church was built in 1902, it was Mrs. Playfair who laid the cornerstone.

Undoubtedly he enjoyed the fruits of his success, but James Playfair certainly enjoyed even more the challenge of a business venture. He was involved in many. In addition to his two Lake fleets, which contained nearly forty vessels, he held interests in salt water shipping, owned a Georgian Bay tug line, and helped to found the Canada Dredge Company. In 1910 he was one of the founders of Midland Drydock Company, which was reorganized as the Midland Shipbuilding Company and in 1916 bought a big lumber mill, tore it down, and constructed a shipyard in its place. The first vessels built were salt water freighters for the Imperial Munitions Board, but the First World War was almost over before any of them were launched. Thereafter the shipyard built mainly Lake freighters for the Playfair fleets. In 1925 he unified all of his shipping trade into one organization, the Great Lakes Navigation Company, but he sold the shipyard and most of his fleet to Canada Steamship Lines the following year.

A series of little vessels of quite a different type operated from the late 1870's, between Midland or Penetanguishene and Parry Sound, carrying freight, cottagers, and round-trip passengers who wanted to see the inside channel of the 30,000 Islands of the North Shore.

In 1921, a group of Midland businessmen bought from Canada Steamship Lines a 152-foot iron sidewheeler that had been in use on the St. Lawrence, renamed her *Midland City,* and put her on the Midland-Parry Sound run. The same year they purchased the 74-foot *City of Dover* and put her in service between Midland and the nearby Honey Harbour resort area.

For a number of years the *Midland City* plied between Midland and Parry Sound. A fast train from Toronto, known as the Flyer, would arrive at Midland about noon, move out on the town dock beside the waiting vessel, which already would be loaded with provisions and merchandise from Midland shops destined for North Shore points, and stand there with locomotive steaming. Passengers would stream across to the ship. After a few minutes of excited activity the train would back away and soon afterwards the *Midland City* would sound her whistle, pull out from the dock, and head up the inside channel. She called at numerous landings along the way and by evening would reach Parry Sound. Next day she returned, arriving at Midland again in the late morning.

In 1933 the steam engine built by Gildersleeve at Kingston in 1870 was removed, as were the paddle wheels, and she was given a twin-screw diesel installation. She continued travelling the inside channel for another fifteen years. Meanwhile cars increased in number, and she usually carried several, for the roads between Midland and Parry Sound were bad and astonishingly indirect. As cars became more commonplace, the fast train was discontinued, its tracks taken up, and a small diesel train that went a roundabout way gave the only rail passenger service to Midland. In time that too stopped. Auto roads also began to reach places along the North Shore that previously had been accessible only by water.

The seventy-year-old boat was showing her age. Despite the heavy planking bolted to the outside of the hull to protect it from rocks, she began to spring leaks whenever she scraped bottom—and at other times as well. Her captain became adept at running her aground in shallow places where she could rest until she was pumped out and patched up. Because of her sheltered route this was not particularly dangerous, but neither was it good. In 1949 her owners became involved in a labour dispute and partly as a result of that sold both her and the *City of Dover* to a Penetanguishene company.

Two other small lines that eventually merged operated on Georgian Bay and Lake Superior. In the early 1900's the wooden propellers *Manitou* and *Caribou* were built at Goderich for the Dominion Transportation Company. Despite its resounding name, the Dominion Transportation Company was a Canadian subsidiary of the Booth Fisheries Corporation of

Chicago, and the main function of its vessels was to carry supplies to the many small fishing villages on the Bay and Lake Superior, and to carry their fish to the nearest rail lines for quick transport to United States markets. But the steamers would also carry whatever else came their way.

Although the company published a timetable, that did not mean a great deal. The captains of the vessels were cautious. This was especially true of Captain Batten of the *Caribou*, who managed each autumn to lose about a week, so that by the end of the season he would be back on schedule again, a week late. The steamers might be delayed by storm, fog, or the smoke of forest fires. There might be sudden changes in schedule. One such change was caused in the early 1930's by a forest fire near Otter Head on Lake Superior. Otter Head became a port of call although it had no docking facilities. Either by pushing their bows against the solid rock shore, or by lightering, the boats unloaded men, equipment, horses, and mules to fight the fire. Passengers were given pails of water and wet mops or brooms, and they patrolled the decks, watching for sparks that might be carried in the heavy clouds of smoke that billowed around the wooden vessels.

As Manitoulin Island developed into a cattle-raising area, the shipment of cattle by water from there to Owen Sound became common. On one occasion the *Caribou* unloaded freight at Gore Bay from her port side, and then moved to the cattle dock to load cattle on her starboard. The animals moved ruminatively aboard, across the deck, and out the port side gangways which still were open. A cattle roundup by rowboat followed. At another time the fireman of the *Manitou* discovered a cow in the fire hold. When he opened the boiler door to throw in some coal, the cow saw the fire, became violent, chased him into the coal bunker, and kept him there. Steam pressure fell. The engineer grew concerned and investigated. Finally he did the only thing he could do—cut a hole in the bulkhead between the fire and cargo holds, and led the animal through and up the freight elevator to rejoin its fellow cows. The fireman went back to shovelling coal, and the ship picked up speed.

143

A syndicate of Owen Sound men formed a competing line, the Owen Sound Transportation Company, and in 1925 they bought a vessel, renamed her the *Manitoulin*, and put her on the run between Owen Sound and the Sault. In 1928 another vessel was added and renamed the *Manasoo*. Competition was vigorous between the two lines. It probably reached its height at the Georgian Bay fishing town of Killarney, where seven hundred to a thousand boxes of trout and whitefish were sent out each trip. On occasion, boats of each line would try to reach the same dock at the same time to pick up the same cargo, bashing fenders, docks, and tempers in the process.

In 1936 the ships of the two lines were placed in a pool and operated by the management of the Owen Sound Company. Soon afterwards the two were combined as the Dominion and Owen Sound Transportation Company, but the clumsy name was soon shortened to just the Owen Sound Transportation Company. The concern then owned four vessels: the *Caribou, Manitou, Manitoulin,* and *Normac.*

With the *Normac* the Owen Sound Co. in the 30's had built up a ferry service between Tobermory and Manitoulin Is. Later she was joined by the *Caribou.* The Normac could take twelve cars; the *Caribou* thirteen. But cars were multiplying like metal rabbits. At times over a hundred and fifty of them would be waiting to get on one of the boats. Sometimes there was a two-day wait, and accommodations at each end of the run were almost nil.

In 1946 the *Caribou* was decommissioned and the company placed in service the steel *Norisle*, 212 feet long, built at Collingwood especially for the Manitoulin ferry service. Running alternate trips with the *Normac* she travelled back and forth between Tobermory and South Baymouth. In 1949 the *Manitoulin* was retired and in 1950 the *Norgoma*, a steel vessel 190 feet long, was delivered by the Collingwood shipyards and put on the North Shore run.

The cargoes on these local runs were extremely diverse. A 1953 *Norgoma* voyage carried barrels, sacks, kegs, and cars. A case of butter was unloaded at Killarney for the general store; a horsedrawn hay rake and a complete set of household furnishings, including the stove, were carried from Cockburn

Island to Thessalon; a large number of new fish boxes was loaded at Gore Bay for delivery to Owen Sound.

The number of autos crossing by ferry service continued to increase, while freight carried by the *Norgoma* along the North Shore steadily decreased. Roads had begun to penetrate to Bay-shore points. In 1962 a road was finally laid to Killarney and that formerly isolated fishing centre could then be reached by car and truck. Summer passengers alone could not support the vessel, and the government, which had subsidized her to a degree, no longer saw reason to continue. During the 1963 season the company announced that the *Norgoma* would end her North Shore-North Channel service and be placed on the Manitoulin ferry run. For the first time in over a century many of the little ports of Georgian Bay would be entirely without steamer service.

The local passenger-and-freight service had boiled down to the Manitoulin ferry run, but the service from Georgian Bay to the head of Lake Superior continued a little longer. The Canadian Pacific Railway still ran the *Assiniboia* and *Keewatin* between Port McNicoll and the head of Lake Superior, carrying both passengers and package freight. At Port Mc-Nicoll the carefully manicured dockside, with green lawns, elaborate flower beds, and little naval cannon, still reminded one traveller of the setting for an English musical comedy of the 20's. The theme of slightly antique British luxury was also carried out aboard the steamers, which after all had been built in Scotland in the days of Empire.

This was the last regularly scheduled passenger service on all of the Great Lakes. The *Athabasca* and *Alberta* had been scrapped during the 1940's, after running as package freighters between Chicago and Port McNicoll from 1938 until the end of 1943. The *Manitoba* was retired in 1949. No new passenger vessels were built. The margin of profit was small in the passenger business, and the C.P.R., like other rail companies, was turning away from it both on land and on water. Then came the tragic burning of the passenger steamer *Noronic* in Toronto harbour, which led the Canadian government to enforce more and more stringent safety measures. The interiors of the two remaining C.P.R. steamers were swathed in automatic sprinkler systems—there were even sprinkler outlets in the clothes lockers off the staterooms—but their days were numbered.

The end came in 1965. The last passenger trip was made by the *Assiniboia*, under Captain Ernest H. Ridd, on November 28th. There were two passengers on board. Both of them were representatives of the Great Lakes Historical Society.

# The pleasure-seekers

Some early tourists on Georgian Bay travelled in a style now hard to achieve. Mrs. Anna Jameson, who came this way in 1837, not only rode in a big canoe manned by *voyageurs* who made camp and cooked for her, but frequently was also carried in and out of the canoe. Mrs. Jameson was fashionably plump, and the man appointed to the task did not always find it easy; he complained to his fellows at length.

Lord Morpeth, seventh Earl of Carlisle, on a tour of Canada in 1842, travelled from Penetanguishene to Manitoulin Island in order to observe the distribution of presents to the Indians there. His party used canoes. One of the *voyageurs* was assigned, as his first duty each day, the preparation of their morning bitters for the Englishmen, and before breakfast he would hear the call from each of the tents in turn, "Louie, are you there? Bring me my cocktail." Morpeth's lordly attitude seems to have extended towards the entire party. One day he was duck-shooting with several others, including Mr. Jarvis, Superintendent of Indian Affairs. He fired at a duck and managed to pepper his companions; several of them, including Jarvis, bled considerably. "Lord Morpeth, what do you mean?" indignantly shouted Jarvis. "You've shot the whole party!" The answer was prompt and frank. "I don't care a damn—I've killed the duck anyhow."

When steamers began to run from Sturgeon Bay to Sault Ste. Marie in the early 1850's, other less distinguished tourists began to travel through Georgian Bay, rubbing elbows with emigrants and traders. When Collingwood became a rail terminus in 1855 and the trains then connected with the steamers, pleasure travel became even easier. The travellers could not only enjoy the scenery but they could also see that the beautiful shores and islands the steamers passed would be fine places to spend a summer holiday.

By 1879 a guidebook published in Toronto could say, "This healthful land-locked offshoot of Lake Huron has long been known as a favourite resort of the tourist." It commented on brook trout fishing at Meaford and on pickerel, maskinonge, and bass fishing at Penetanguishene and Waubaushene. Another book published five years later reported that "no finer flavoured fish exist than those which inhabit the waters of the Muskoka Lakes and the Georgian Bay." It mentioned Wasaga Beach, a great favourite and a quiet resort, which had "fine white sand, so hard that the wheels of the vehicle scarcely make an indentation, smooth, and without a stone," and added, "should youthful spirits incline to the vivacious, what can afford a greater sensation of pleasure than a drive in a good rig, behind a fine blooded and spirited horse." Of the North Shore it said, "Numbers of the islands have already been purchased by private individuals, both Canadian and American, who have erected their residences and beautified their surroundings according to their various tastes and inclinations. Numbers of gentlemen camp on the islands during the summer."

T. Long & Brother of Collingwood advertised camping supplies in this book. The Seguin House, at Parry Sound, appealed to a different taste by describing its spacious grounds and croquet lawns. The Georgian Bay House, Penetanguishene, had something for everyone: a "table replete with the best to be obtained," lovely scenery, pure cool breezes, boating without danger, the best fishing on the continent, an excellent livery, and drives and "pic-nic" parties. Its rates were from $1.00 to $2.50 per day.

148

In the early 80's houseboats began to appear on Georgian Bay. These craft, which consisted of wooden houses built on large scows, were pulled by steam tugs to sheltered places among the islands and anchored there. An early builder and operator was the Palace Houseboat Co., of Midland. Two of its largest boats, the *Hiawatha* and *Iona*, were much in demand, especially by American tourists.

There were a number of summer homes, some of them quite elaborate, on the North Shore islands by the mid-80's. One B. F. Jones even owned two islands, on each of which he had built extensive apiaries for bees that he had imported from the Holy Land and from Italy; to this day they are known as Palestine Island and Jones Island. The general area remained quite wild however, with no roads, railways, or telegraph lines within miles. So even though luxuries could be found in places, the Bay also attracted visitors who loved more rugged outdoor living. An account of a ten-hour trip by four canoemen from Parry Sound to Muskoka, published in 1896, described the wild country through which they passed, but it mentioned also that they saw enroute two or three large parties of Americans, one group of six from the Toronto Canoe Club, and three parties from various places in Muskoka.

One family of commercial fishermen—two brothers and a sister who had come originally from Scotland—decided to cater to tourists rather than follow the hard and chancy calling in which they began. At first they simply accommodated a few visitors in their fishing camp on one of the more attractive of the Thirty Thousand Islands. Their fame spread by word of mouth however, and in time they had to put up another building for their guests; then there were additions; and finally came a fifty-room hotel.

About 1896 appeared a little book with a big title, *Guide to the Muskoka Lakes, Upper Maganetawan & Inside Channel of the Georgian Bay*, which offered vacationists one way to reach North Shore points.

> The first class upper cabin paddle steamer, "F. B. Maxwell," makes daily trips in close connection with the Northern Division of the Grand Trunk Railway at Penetanguishene, and Midland, to Parry Sound over the justly

famous inside route. The staunch propeller "Imperial" makes semi-weekly trips as far as Byng Inlet and French River. . . . These steamers have stateroom accommodation for passengers, and the fishing along their route is unexcelled in fresh water.

There began to form along the North Shore summer colonies made up of people who had similar interests. In 1898 the Madawaska Club, composed of faculty members from the University of Toronto, established itself at Go-Home Bay. It erected a clubhouse; members camped on nearby islands and later built cottages on them. The fishing was excellent, and the place was known for the fine pickerel and bass that were caught there.

During a cruise on Georgian Bay in 1898 the American yacht *Belle Marie* put in at Little Current. The mills that had formerly sustained the place were idle because of the American tariff on lumber, and it then seemed to exist largely on "the tourist and huckleberry business." There were three hotels at that time, and when one of the yachtsmen asked the village baker if any summer people came there, he was told, with unconscious but staggering exaggeration, "Why, more come here than anywhere else."

In the spring of 1899, *Forest and Stream*, then a leading outdoor publication, printed the design by J. Wilton Morse, Esq., of Toronto, of a 12-foot sailing dinghy that had been built for vacation sailing on Georgian Bay and that had proved successful there. This was the beginning of a popular racing class. Dinghies filled the need of cottagers for little boats that could be sailed or rowed for pleasure or utility, and they caught on quickly. Soon dinghy sailing was a frequent sport along the North Shore. The sailing dinghy and the Collingwood Mackinaw share honours as the two small craft particularly identified with Georgian Bay.

Sailing dinghies were especially attractive to young people. The skipper of one of them, a teen-age girl who had as crew another teen-age girl, one day found her way blocked by a large raft of logs being pulled at a snail's pace by a steam tug. The tug had just passed; behind it was the big raft surrounded by a restraining boom of logs chained together. At the rate the raft was moving it might be an hour before the way was clear. But the boom was a little longer than necessary and as a result the logs forming the raft within it had sagged back, leaving thirty feet or so of open water inside the boom at the front end, where the tow line was made fast. The young skipper saw this open water directly ahead of her, and she drove her boat under full sail directly for one of the big logs of the boom. As she bore down on it she commanded "centre board up" to her crew; up came the board, the dinghy slid onto the slowly moving log, teetered, and was over, to the accompaniment of anguished yells from the tug. "Board down," she said, and the little boat scooted across the fringe of open water just ahead of the on-coming log raft. As they came to the boom on the far side she again said "board up," and again the boat slid across the boom; "board down," she said, and they sailed away, waving as the tug crew shook their fists.

By the early 1900's, summer cottages were appearing at some of the more isolated spots on the Bay. At Pointe au Baril, between Parry Sound and Byng Inlet, there were several cottages in 1903, when Hamilton Davis, a Rochester man, became so enthusiastic about the place that he decided to build a summer hotel, the Ojibway, on an island offshore. He had to muster the help of the scattered residents for miles around, plus that of some of the Indians from the nearby Shawanaga Reservation, but all pitched in to construct a typical frame summer hotel of the period. It opened its doors in 1906. Access was entirely by water; neither roads nor railroads passed anywhere near.

The first guests at the Ojibway came mainly from the States, as did most of the cottagers in that particular area during the early years of the century. The Americans liked to emphasize the wilderness atmosphere, gave Indian names to their cottages, and wore old clothes. In sharp contrast were those Canadians who came there a bit later, and brought with them neatly uniformed housemaids. The men often wore neckties, and one Canadian, to the consternation of his American neighbours, even brought his own bagpiper.

151

From 1900 to the First World War the North Shore offered a very pleasant kind of holiday life. This was a time of prosperity and comfort for the well-to-do and the middle class. Some of the North Shore vacationists used tents and canoes, but others had fine homes and yachts. Most owned some sort of cottage and some sort of boat, and all had enough leisure to be there. They came by train to Midland, Penetang, or Parry Sound, and went on to the islands on vessels of the regular coasting lines or in their own craft. They passed their time in fishing, swimming, canoeing, or sailing; in sketching and painting; or in having neighbours over for tea and perhaps a game of cards. The life was as graceful and unhurried as the steam yachts that passed among the islands. During these last Edwardian years, the summer residents of the North Shore set a pattern of vacation living that has been copied, as nearly as the times would allow, by every generation that has followed. Even the businessman who flies in today in his own or his company's plane for a weekend of fishing is not trying to break the pattern, but rather to enjoy what part of it he can.

Some of the Georgian Bay summer hotels were almost clubs. The same people came every year, everyone knew everyone else, and unless a new guest was properly introduced he found the social climate distinctly chilly. Few people were able to retaliate as neatly as did two young and innocent ladies who discovered themselves in such a situation during the 1920's.

It happened at a large and ornate, wooden structure that reposed on an island along the shore between Midland and Parry Sound. Those who came every year were conservative people from the more conservative Ontario cities. Usually they arrived in their own boats, which then lay at the hotel dock; occasionally someone of unchallenged social position might, without causing raised eyebrows, come on the coasting steamer that stopped twice daily. Their recreations were most genteel, and the high point of the day, at least for the ladies, was afternoon tea on the big front porch. There they all gathered with hampers filled with delicacies prepared by the kitchen and with a few select added items brought with them from the city; there they all sat amidst the polite tinkling of china and silverware; and there they exchanged bits of choice gossip and samples of their rarer viands while they watched the boats pass to and fro.

On one such afternoon a battered hired launch from Parry Sound chugged up to the dock under their observant eyes. In it were the two young ladies and their luggage. They had come from the States, and having heard that this hotel was typically Canadian they had decided that it would be more interesting than one that catered especially to Americans. Arriving in Parry Sound on a Sunday, when the coastal steamers did not run, they had hired the one available launch.

The boatman saw his passengers and cargo safely on the hotel dock and then swung his craft about and headed back up the channel. The two girls, who were somewhat dishevelled from their rough and windy trip in an open boat, looked at the hotel, from which no welcoming person appeared, looked at their luggage, and looked at each other. Then they picked up the bags and trudged the length of the dock, past the silently watchful front porch, and in to the hotel desk. There, since they did have reservations, a silent and superior clerk permitted them to register and a silent and disapproving porter led them to their room.

Word passed quickly along the front porch that the new-comers were Americans! What was more, they came from a small midwestern college where, as members of the faculty, they actually worked! When the two of them came back to the porch in a little while, all heads turned the other way. The girls sat alone, in outer darkness. Not for them a kind word, let alone the offer of a cherished English biscuit or a dab of Scottish jelly. Only grudgingly the management, as a great favour, provided teapot and cups.

At the end of a thoroughly unhappy week, during which they were snubbed at every turn, the two young women set out to visit friends in Midland. They had been invited to spend the night there, and looked forward to it with relief from what they had been enduring. They boarded the steamer, rode down the shore, and were met at the town dock by their Midland friends.

That evening the friends had a party. Among those present were the James Playfairs; he was one of the leading citizens of

Midland and by then his influence reached well beyond the Georgian Bay region. Mrs. Playfair was greatly taken with the two young ladies, they in turn found her a sympathetic listener, and before long out poured the whole story of their miserable week at the summer hotel. She was quite interested. When were they returning? Next day on the steamer. Not at all—they would go back on the *Venetia*, the Playfair yacht. The girls protested feebly. Mrs. Playfair was adamant; they were returning on the yacht.

Next afternoon the *Venetia*, a considerably larger vessel than the coastal steamer, carefully felt her way in to the hotel dock with every flag flying, including the burgee of a distinguished yacht club. There was a rustle of anticipation on the front porch; this was an event. The yacht moved slowly in. Uniformed sailors made her fast while other uniformed sailors put out a gangway and stood at attention. A little group of people said their farewells on deck; then two of the group came ashore, escorted by a ship's officer. They were the two young ladies who, a week before, had arrived out of nowhere in a hired launch.

Trying hard to look nonchalant, they walked up the dock, followed by sailors carrying their overnight bags. When they were half way, there suddenly was a loud report from the little saluting cannon at the bow of the yacht. This almost spoiled the whole effect; they both leaped involuntarily. "Don't look around," one hissed to the other, and they proceeded on, past the front porch with its gaping audience. The hotel porter scurried to take the bags from the sailors and rushed ahead of the young ladies to their room. He bowed out, almost bumping his head on the floor. When he was gone they collapsed on their beds, burying their heads under their pillows so that their laughter would not ring through the whole hotel.

They had two days of vacation left and they decided to make the most of it. That evening three different people introduced themselves; the girls were politely distant. At breakfast several elderly ladies smiled and nodded; the girls did not see them. When tea time came there was a round of invitations to share the contents of the hampers; the girls were not hungry, thank you. They snubbed every overture until they took their departure aboard the daily steamer, with the hotel porter standing at the dockside, bowing, and the genteel ladies on the front porch looking wistful.

Since World War I the North Shore has grown less isolated and less wild; roads, cars, and more and more people have reached it. Coastal steamers have gone, small motor boats have come and have multiplied, and aeroplanes have appeared. But the Shore still attracts fishermen seeking bass and maskinonge, the islands still offer relative isolation, and one still can find either wilderness camping sites or large homes and good hotels.

The maintenance of a summer home in a wilderness area, possibly on an island, many miles from one's regular abode is a project fraught with complications. Lucky is the cottager who can use one of his hobbies to solve some of his problems. Such a man is a Columbus, Ohio, attorney, Freeman T. Eagleson II, a railroad buff who owns Round Island in the North Channel.

The Eagleson family has built an extensive, if rustic, establishment there—a power house, storage shed, 625-gallon water tank, and workshop, all located adjacent to the log house. There is a rise of some fifty feet between the island dock and the house. Up it must be carried all supplies, including tanks of propane cooking gas and drums of gasoline. The obvious solution—to the owner, at least—was a small railroad.

The Round Island Line has over 600 feet of eighteen-inch gauge track, and more is planned. Eagleson designed the locomotive, which is driven by a three-horsepower engine, and had the essential parts made by a metal-working firm at Sault Ste. Marie. He also has two flat cars, each of which can carry 400 pounds or a fifty-five-gallon drum of gasoline. Downhill the little train can travel at twenty-five miles per hour.

During the summer, Eagleson frequently commutes from his home in Columbus to his home on Round Island. The trip involves four different kinds of transportation. He travels to the Columbus airport by car; from there he flies in his own small jet plane to the landing strip at Gore Bay, Manitoulin

Island; and he goes on to his island by motor boat. The last 600-odd feet of the trip are, of course, by rail.

Until after World War I the beaches of Georgian Bay, lying between Collingwood and Midland, were largely undeveloped. Wasaga Beach did attract some people who came by rail to Collingwood and then drove to the beach, but it still could honestly claim to be a quiet resort. Some of the other beaches had a few cottages, belonging mostly to people in the nearby towns. Still others were completely deserted.

As the auto came more and more on the scene, and the growing population of Canada and America found it increasingly easy to drive to Georgian Bay, the beaches developed quickly. As the hydro-electric power system grew, the ready availability of electricity for lighting, cooking, pumping water, and heating made them even more attractive to the vacationer. By the beginning of World War II most of the beaches were well built up.

Local businesses learned to adapt themselves during the summer months to the tourist trade. In one town was a small hotel that catered extensively to summer visitors. Flower boxes were at the leaded glass windows and the rooms inside were crowded with antique bric-a-brac, some of it quite valuable. The proprietors were two gnomish brothers who bustled about, welcoming guests and supervising the excellent dining room. The atmosphere of the place attracted elderly ladies; the good steaks at moderate prices brought parents with growing families. It was a favourite spot for family Sunday dinners. Housewives from nearby summer colonies did the family grocery shopping in that particular town just so that they could lunch at the little hotel. On occasion cottagers came from thirty miles away. The place was a summer institution. Probably the elderly ladies enjoyed it most; certainly they were the most horrified when, one spring, word went round that the police had closed the little hotel the preceding winter for being a house of prostitution.

The growth of beaches continues to this day. On many beaches extra streets have now been opened for additional cottages, and more distant beaches, such as the one on Christian

Island, have been made accessible. Most beaches now have cottagers' associations that try to solve the problems caused by the steady increase in population. They work out rules about such things as how close to bathing areas water skiers may disport themselves, and they also try to influence local authorities in matters that affect resorters. The talent available to these groups is often impressive. A recent president of the Thunder Beach Association, for example, was Mr. Justice Wishart F. Spence, of the Supreme Court of Canada.

Not only are more people coming to the beaches in summer, but a small though growing number returns now in winter. Many of the newer cottages are comfortable in cold weather and many beach roads are kept free of snow except during the heaviest storms. Georgian Bay towns have long promoted winter carnivals, and a sizable ski resort area has developed in recent years near Collingwood, but the use of beach cottages for cold weather recreation has little direct connection with these activities. Whatever skiing or tobogganing people do at their cottages on a winter weekend is as casual and as little organized as the swimming or boating they do there in summer.

Local residents have learned to accept winter vacationists as calmly as they do those who come in summer. Late one Friday night a car full of girls bound through a snow storm for a beach cottage finally slid to a halt some twenty miles from their destination. They got out and walked around the car. Obviously they could go no farther until the snow plow passed. A short distance away loomed a farmhouse; the group took their sleeping bags from the car and made their way to it. Wind swooped around the unlighted house. There was no doorbell and the sound of their knocking on the front door was lost in the noise of the storm. One of them tried the door. It was unlocked. After a whispered consultation they entered, stepping into the farm living room and closing the door behind them. Outside the wind blew. Dimly they could make out their surroundings. They unrolled their sleeping bags on the floor, climbed into them, and went to sleep. There the farm family discovered them next morning and, not greatly surprised, fed them breakfast and sent them on their way.

157

# Today

The people at Collingwood build the largest ships on the Great Lakes, 730-footers, the longest that can pass through the St. Lawrence Seaway. A few miles off in one direction are the Blue Mountain ski resorts, the most elaborate on the Bay; a few miles in the opposite direction lies Wasaga, largest and most active of Georgian Bay beaches. Industry and sport on the Bay are side by side. The industrial centres are not large, although they are surprisingly potent. Only Owen Sound is officially a city, and it has less than 20,000 people. Urban sprawl has started on the fringes of the larger places, but so far it has not overwhelmed the landscape. Split levels do not yet outnumber the red brick houses with front porches. Because the towns are small the countryside is close at hand. Also because of their size, their manufacturing capacity is not often evident to holiday visitors. The visitors themselves are one of the largest sources of income for the Bay region, and local Chambers of Commerce wisely emphasize outdoor recreation instead of industrial production—except when speaking to industrialists.

As a result, visitors sometimes get the impression that the Bay area is nothing but undeveloped wilderness. At times events reinforce this idea. There was, for example, a distinguished United States senator who came to the North Shore via Sault Ste. Marie in an elegant American car of prestigious make. His road carried him through none of the big towns. After he arrived at the wildest part of the Bay shore, the transmission of his car failed. He found a garage with only a little difficulty, but it then developed that transmissions for that exotic car were not to be had in Canada. The car finally went back to the United States behind a tow truck. Its owner now conceives Georgian Bay to lie in the darkest jungle on the North American continent.

Most vacationists have happier experiences. The best-known vacation areas are probably the North Shore, the beaches, and Manitoulin Island, but the Counties of Grey and Bruce have many attractions. The Blue Mountains west of Collingwood, which provide the slopes that attract world-famous skiers, could be mountains only in flat terrain; elsewhere they would be only steep hills. They do, however, also offer the summer visitor some rugged vacation areas, waterfalls, trout streams, and hiking trails. Throughout the Bruce the streams and lakes and shores draw fishermen seeking trout and bass. Tourists with fond memories of the dog story *Beautiful Joe,* by Marshall Saunders, can make a sentimental pause at the small park in Meaford that surrounds the grave of the original Beautiful Joe. At Meaford also is a yard that builds fine sailing yachts and that can make emergency repairs for visiting sailors who find themselves in trouble.

Yachtsmen get a better view of Georgian Bay than most travellers. Yachts from the United States usually put in at Tobermory at the harbour called the Big Tub—to distinguish it from the smaller and more commercial Little Tub nearby— making fast to rings attached to the rock shore. They also usually visit Little Current, where the town dock lies beside a small park, near the village main street, across which are stores that sell everything from imported luxury goods to Canadian hardware. Little Current is a place where men and women from shiny mahogany, glass, and chrome motor cruisers rub shoulders with the well-worn seadogs off famous sailing racers. Killarney, the old fishing town, is also a favourite port of call for cruisers from the States. In these harbours—the Tub, Little Current, and Killarney—American yachts far out-number the Canadian ones. Many go no farther into the Bay, however, and thus miss a good deal of its charm. At the southern end of Georgian Bay, Canadian yachts predominate, most of them craft with home ports on these shores, whose owners come from the Bay towns or from Toronto and other nearby cities.

Ann Davison, the Englishwoman who crossed the Atlantic alone in a 23-foot sloop in 1953, later visited Georgian Bay. She came in a small motor cruiser through the Trent Waterway from Lake Ontario, and her first reaction was that the shores of Georgian Bay are not those of a lake, but are seashores—wild, northern seashores. Her cruise through the Bay was typical of what may be done here in a small yacht. She discovered that Honey Harbour was difficult to reach but attractive enough to repay the effort. She found the Inside Channel up the North Shore to be scenic and sheltered, but in places not well marked. She thought Killarney looked like one of the bleaker northern coasts. And she was stormbound in Meldrum Bay. All of which are things that might enliven the cruises of many less experienced yachtsmen.

The beaches of the Bay vary widely in character. Wasaga fosters an amusement-park atmosphere, with ferris wheels and bingo games. It is the largest beach, a beautiful length of sand which is a bit nerve-wracking to the uninitiated, for people, cars, buses, horses, bicycles, boats, and even aeroplanes may come at you from unexpected angles. After the first day, however, you develop a sense akin to radar and automatically jump in the right direction at the right time.

Eastward from Wasaga along fifty miles of irregular shoreline are the other beaches. Generally speaking, the farther east you go, the quieter and less commercial they get. One of the most pleasant is the small harbour of Thunder Bay, which combines a good yacht anchorage with an attractive sand beach. American visitors sometimes are startled to learn that in the mid-nineteenth century this was a port for disreputable small craft smuggling liquor from the United States into Canada. Casks were hidden in the sand and a tavern keeper from Penetang, who objected to Canadian taxes, would later pick them up. In more recent years the trade moved in the other direction. During the time of Prohibition in the United States, Thunder Bay had not yet become the settled place it now is. Then strange vessels arrived by night, and signal lamps flashed back and forth before the boats came ashore to load.

The people of Georgian Bay are beginning to see that history has commercial value, historic places being tourist attractions, and the small, dedicated band of history enthusiasts are becoming more able to gather money that will provide adequate markers for historic sites and build local museums. The most important and impressive historical place on the Bay is the reconstructed mission fort of Sainte Marie. Professor Wilfrid Jury of the University of Western Ontario supervised both the archaeological exploration of the site and the reconstruction of the mission, rebuilt through the combined efforts of the Jesuit order and the Province of Ontario. It now is under provincial control. Sainte Marie stands again beside the River Wye, as it did in the days of the martyred French missionaries.

The *Nancy*, relic of the War of 1812, was raised from the Nottawasaga River some years ago, largely through the efforts of C. H. J. Snider, the Toronto marine historian, and placed inside a special building on the island that had formed around the hulk. Today there is a general marine museum on the island, which is reached by a short bridge from Wasaga Beach.

At Penetanguishene the stone quarters used by the bachelor officers of the old military post have been turned into a museum, some of the old buildings that once stood nearby have been reconstructed by Dr. Jury, and the locations have been marked for many of the others.

A showplace of Penetanguishene is the little Anglican church, St. James-on-the-Lines, so named because it stood on a street of soldiers' houses. A visitor can amuse himself here by reading old tombstones to his heart's content. Inside the church is a broad aisle, built to allow the soldiers to march in in column of fours. On one wall is a tablet carved of wood, half of which is blank; the inscribed half is to the memory of a lieutenant of the 66th Regiment, "frozen to death on his return from the village after a night of festivity." The blank half was ordered by the commander, as a warning to other merry-makers that it was waiting for them.

A slightly later period of history is represented at the opposite end of Georgian Bay, at Manitowaning on Manitoulin Island, by a museum containing relics of the Indian establishment that the white man gave and then took away; elsewhere in the village are old buildings of some interest. One of the best collections of pioneer tools in Ontario is in the Huronia Museum at Midland, which has excellent displays housed in a handsome new building. Mementoes of the booming steamer days are found in the Collingwood museum, located in the old railway station. Most places on Georgian Bay now realize that they have a history and have begun to do something about it.

The great religious centre of the Georgian Bay region, one which attracts thousands of pilgrims each year, is the Martyrs' Shrine. It is a tall, twin-spired, stone church that looks down on Sainte Marie from the hill that served as a lookout for the early missionaries, and is dedicated to the eight Jesuit martyrs who were killed in the Great Lakes region between 1640 and 1650. In 1930 Pope Pius XI canonized the martyrs, who became the first saints of North America. Now pilgrims and tourists come each year to climb the hill to the church and to see the collection of crutches, canes, braces, and even spectacles left behind by the faithful who have been cured there.

Some fifteen miles from the Shrine as the seagulls fly is the tiny village of Lafontaine. This modern French-Canadian settlement is in the middle of the country so familiar to the French missionaries and explorers, but it's off the usual path of tourists. Here old people and children speak no English, and others speak it only when they do business with outsiders. The village is the centre of a French farming area and the location of the parish church. Some of the older houses are true *habitant* cabins, made of squared logs which formerly were whitewashed every spring to preserve them. Today, however, most of these handsome examples of frontier architecture have been covered by modern imitation brick siding.

Like Georgian Bay itself, the village is an odd combination of old and new. Many of its farmers are well-to-do and use modern methods. It has a well-organized farmers' cooperative,

162

which was founded and encouraged by a forward-looking parish priest. Some of the younger generation show a fondness for current hit tunes and prefer them to more traditional songs, but so far there is no great indication that Anglo-American civilization is breaking up this French community; it only seems to develop it. On long winter nights when the snow outside is deep, they still tell stories that came from France in the sixteen-hundreds, and the *loup garou*, the French werewolf, skirts the edge of the town.

Towards the end of summer the big grain boats start running from the Lakehead to Georgian Bay ports. Before the St. Lawrence Seaway was opened in 1959, the owners of Georgian Bay elevators had a profitable business in transferring grain cargoes that came from the head of the Lakes into rail cars for carriage to the lower St. Lawrence or the east coast. Now, however, freighters carry grain from the Lakehead directly through the Seaway to Montreal and ports farther east. In 1958 over a million tons of wheat were unloaded at Midland; by 1962 that figure had dropped to about 455,000. The grain that now comes into Georgian Bay is largely for consumption in the surrounding areas, but some is for storage in the big elevators. Ships full of grain also come at the end of navigation each year to lie through the winter as floating storage warehouses.

Not much is shipped out of any of these ports, except that at Depot Harbour they load iron ore mined near Sudbury. Other cargoes arriving on the Bay are petroleum products and coal. Petroleum comes mainly to Parry Sound and Britt. Coal is unloaded at Owen Sound, Midland, and Little Current. Coal and oil from the North Shore ports go to industry in the Sudbury district and to railroads, industry, and individual consumers throughout the large area north and east of the Bay.

Towns large enough to have commercial harbours also have sewage problems, although most of them don't seem to realize it. A visiting yachtsman, blundering into the wrong part of the harbour—or in some places, just into the harbour itself—may be overwhelmed by the evidence. Ironically, he may also be prosecuted if he flushes his own head into that same water

163

without giving the sewage adequate treatment. Since World War II, the population of the Georgian Bay region has grown considerably; there is no reason to suppose that it will not continue to grow. In time there may be sizable cities on the Bay shore. One or two of them, pouring sewage and industrial waste into the Bay, could soon change the sparkling drinking water found in most places into the stagnant sludge of a Lake Erie. If these cities expanded industrially along its shores, they could turn them into bleak copies of the New Jersey marshes. This is the kind of thing that may happen before anyone realizes it; one can only hope that the proper authorities are alert.

Manufacturing on Georgian Bay seems infinitely varied. The town of Nobel, near Parry Sound, produces explosives. Collingwood and Thornbury pack vegetables and fruit. Collingwood also makes pottery and china. Owen Sound produces machinery ranging from food choppers through diesel engines to fireboats, not forgetting also the machinery it has built for the largest paper mill in the world, located on Lake Superior. At Midland several companies make high pressure, high temperature, and other hydraulic equipment. Wiarton manufactures small electric motors. Textiles are woven at Meaford. Penetang makes shoes. This is only a sampling. Furniture, wire rope, paint, auto seat covers, fiberglass, electrical equipment—you name it, and you'll probably find it being made somewhere on the Bay.

Products made on Georgian Bay range from the small, precise cameras, lenses, and optical instruments of Ernst Leitz (Canada) Limited, at Midland, to the big, rugged freighters launched by the Collingwood Shipyards. The Leitz factory was established by its parent German company in 1952. There have been shipyards in Collingwood since 1883; the first steel ship, the 308-foot *Huronic*, was launched there in 1901, and the history of the present shipyard is perhaps best dated from that year. Products of these two organizations represent the new and the traditional on Georgian Bay.

The Midland firm, whose president is Günther Leitz, makes optical equipment that is used in over eighty countries. The most famous things it produces are Leica cameras and camera lenses, direct descendants of the first 35 mm camera in the world, the Leica that was introduced in 1924. Many of the newest and most interesting lenses now made by Leitz—telephoto, wide-angle, and high-speed optics—were designed at Midland. The factory there produces mainly items developed by its own experts. Raw optical glass, imported from Germany, is ground and polished into lens elements and then assembled, using Canada balsam for cement and the metal lens mounts that also are manufactured in the Midland factory.

The Collingwood Shipyards are the only ones operating on the Bay. The yards at Midland have produced little since a burst of activity in the 1950's and now they stand abandoned. There is a yard at Owen Sound that launches tugs and barges for both Great Lakes and salt water use, and there are many plants around the Bay that build smaller craft. But only at Collingwood these days are ships built.

Collingwood Shipyards are now a division of Canadian Shipbuilding & Engineering Ltd., which also has the yards at Port Arthur on Lake Superior, and at Kingston on Lake Ontario. Naval architects, engineers, and draftsmen at Collingwood do the design work for the other two yards as well. The Collingwood yards also make such things as mooring winches, hatch clamps, sea valves, hydraulic equipment, and a range of landlubberly items such as 25,000-gallon oil storage tanks. The shipyards are the biggest thing in Collingwood, a town of 8,500, employing about a thousand people.

Through two World Wars the Collingwood yards launched vessels to be manned by allied sailors. During World War II, they built some thirty corvettes, mine sweepers, armed trawlers, and other vessels for the Canadian, British, and United States government. Between the wars and since, they have produced a great variety of ships: tankers, package freighters, even some passenger vessels. But the one type that has been launched most regularly over the years is the bulk freighter. The second vessel built at the present yard was the *Agawa*, a 377-foot bulk freight steamer, delivered in 1902; one of the most recent launchings, in 1966, was that of the 730-foot multi-diesel bulk carrier *Simcoe*, of Canada Steamship Lines.

The *Simcoe* is big. Everything about her is big. One wonders what the gallant Captain Peter M. Campbell, one of the founders of the shipyard, would think of a vessel that so dwarfs the crack steamers he commanded. Each of the *Simcoe*'s three anchors weighs 12,000 pounds. The ship's main propulsion consists of four twelve-cylinder diesel engines, producing a total of 8,000 horsepower. If in addition the two engines that normally drive her electric generators are connected by pneumatic clutches to the shafts of the main engines, the total horsepower available is more than 9,000. The *Simcoe*'s cargo holds carry over a million bushels. Her seventeen steel hatch covers are handled by her own electric travelling gantry crane that runs on tracks on the spar deck. Because of her length she has a bow steering propeller driven by an 800-horsepower electric motor. Building a ship of this size is not an unusual feat at Collingwood. In 1965 the yard delivered the *Tarantau*, a self-unloader that also was 730 feet long. Her equipment will unload 4,200 tons of coal or 6,000 tons of stone per hour. On October 10th, 1967, another 730-foot bulk freighter, *Feux-Follets*, was christened at Collingwood. More, perhaps even larger, will follow.

Driving west from Collingwood, past the ski resorts with their *ersatz* Swiss architecture and one of the ski lifts that runs also in summer to give tourists a thrill, you come into the apple country of Georgian Bay, which centres about the town of Thornbury. The County of Grey is also one of the biggest livestock producers in Ontario. Agriculture is important everywhere on the Bay except along the North Shore. Dairy and egg production is high in both Grey and Bruce Counties. Tobacco is raised in Bruce. Manitoulin Island and Simcoe County, at opposite ends of the Bay, are both agricultural. The products of Manitoulin are much like those of Bruce and Grey, but Simcoe County is a little different. Over one-quarter of all the potatoes grown in Ontario are raised in the Georgian Bay region, and two thirds of those come from Simcoe County. In the whole region over 20% of the labour force is directly engaged in agriculture, and well over half of the people live in rural areas.

Many waves have broken on the shore since lumber was king of the Bay. Now less than 1% of the labour force is engaged in forestry and less than 5% of it in the wood and furniture industries. The remaining forests, however, are still an economic asset. In the more settled counties of Simcoe, Grey, and Bruce, about a quarter of the area is forested, mostly in small wood-lots; many of these are attached to farms. Much of the wood produced here is used for local building or goes to the nearby furniture factories. The growing of Christmas trees, mainly for export to the United States, centres about Penetanguishene. Along the North Shore there is considerable second-growth forest; little else will grow there. Some wood from this area goes also to the furniture factories, but much of it is good only for manufacture into wood pulp or particle board. It is a far, sad cry from the days of the 80's and 90's when the red sash brigade tramped the woods and the mill chimneys rose above the towns.

The only unchanging things on Georgian Bay are the waves and the winds. The past moves into the present and the present into the future. Fort Sainte Marie, rebuilt, lies a stone's-throw from a new electronics factory. The ghosts of schooners running before the west wind meet the visions of thousand-foot-long freighters not yet on the drawing boards.

The first explorers and traders came this way. Fur, lumber, and grain have passed east through the Bay; settlers for the midwestern United States and for prairie Canada have travelled west. The War of 1812 and the Red River Rebellion have affected the area. Ships launched here have sailed every Great Lake and several oceans. Recreational facilities have developed all around the Bay, and thousands of American and Canadian tourists have come to know and love the area. Its vivid and contrasting moods have inspired countless artists. Truly this is the sixth Great Lake.

# Bibliography and Notes

## Abbreviations Used

*AA—American Antiquity*
*CGJ—Canadian Geographical Journal*
*CHR—Canadian Historical Review*
*DMH—Detroit Marine Historian*
*IS—Inland Seas*
*MD—Mer Douce*
ODLF—Ontario Department of Lands and Forests
*OH—Ontario History*
OPA—Ontario Provincial Archives
PAC—Public Archives of Canada
*PP—Pioneer Papers*, Simcoe County Pioneer and Historical Society
*PR—Papers and Records*, Ontario Historical Society
TBHS—Thunder Bay Historical Society
*TRSC—Transactions of the Royal Society of Canada*

## Prologue

Consul W. Butterfield, *History of Brulé's Discoveries and Explorations*, (Cleveland, 1898) and J. H. Cranston, *Etienne Brulé, Immortal Scoundrel* (Toronto, 1949), give book-length accounts of Brulé's foibles and accomplishments. H. R. Holmden, *Catalogue of Maps and Charts in the Map Room of the Dominion Archives* (Ottawa, 1912), lists "A Plan of the Straits from Lake Huron into the Manitoulin Lake from the Open Gap to Cabot's Head," from a survey made 26th, 27th, and 28th September, 1815, by W. F. W. Owen. Gabriel Sagard, *The Long Journey to the Country of the Hurons*, (Toronto, 1939; George M. Wrong, ed.; edition of 1632).

Scattered references to Brulé appear in many of the basic sources for Chapter I; they are pulled together in the two volumes about him that are listed above. Other references for this Prologue appear later, under the appropriate chapters.

## Huron Harvest

Basic material is in the following. *Samuel de Champlain's Works* (Toronto,

1929; H. P. Biggar, ed.). J. F. Jameson (ed.), *Narratives of New Nether-lands* (New York, 1907). E. B. O'Callaghan (ed.), *Documents Relative to the Colonial History of the State of New York* (Albany, 1856). Sagard, *op. cit.* Reuben G. Thwaites (ed.), *The Jesuit Relations and Allied Documents, 1610-1791* (Cleveland, 1896-1901).

Among the best archaeological descriptions are these: William Sherwood Fox and Wilfrid Jury, *Saint Ignace, Canadian Cradle of Martyrdom* (Toronto, 1949). Arthur E. Jones, *Old Huronia*, Report of the Bureau of Archives, 1908 (Toronto, 1909). Elsie McLeod Jury, "Indian Village and Mission Sites of Huronia," *CGJ*, LXVII (1963). Wilfrid Jury and Elsie McLeod Jury, *Sainte Marie Among the Hurons* (Toronto, 1954). T. F. McIlwraith, *Archaeological Work in Huronia, 1946: Excavations Near Warminster*, U. of Toronto, n.d. Frank Ridley, "A Search for Ossossane and its Environs," *OH*, XXIX (1947).

Interpretative material is found in many references. H. P. Biggar, *The Early Trading Companies of New France* (Toronto, 1901). Morris Bishop, *Champlain, the Life of Fortitude* (New York, 1948). Bernard DeVoto, *The Course of Empire* (Boston, 1952). George T. Hunt, *The Wars of the Iroquois* (Madison, 1940). Harold A. Innes, *The Fur Trade in Canada* (New Haven, 1930). C. C. James, "The Downfall of the Huron Nation," *TRSC*, Second Series, 1906-1907, XII, Sec. II. Diamond Jenness, *The Indians of Canada* (Ottawa, 1934). W. V. Kinietz, *The Indians of the Western Great Lakes* (Ann Arbor, 1940). Jean E. Murray, "The Fur Trade in New France and New Netherland," *CHR* XIX (1938). E. B. O'Callaghan, *History of New Netherland* (New York, 1846). Francis Parkman, *The Jesuits of North America* and *Pioneers of France in the New World* (Cambridge, Mass., 1872). Elisabeth Tooker, *An Ethnography of the Huron Indians* (Midland, 1967) (Reprint of Bulletin 190 of the Bureau of American Ethnology, Washington, 1964). Daniel Wilson, "The Huron—Iroquois of Canada, a Typical Race of American Aborigines," *TRSC* II, Sec. II (1884). George M. Wrong, *The Rise and Fall of New France* (New York, 1928).

There were three Fathers Lalemant in New France at about the same time. They have sometimes been confused. Charles Lalemant was Superior of the Quebec Mission from 1625 to 1627, when he returned to France. In 1633 he came back to Quebec, where he was closely associated with Champlain, whom he attended at his death, returning permanently to France in 1639. Jerome, brother of Charles, was Superior of the Huron Missions from 1638 to 1644. Their nephew, Gabriel, came to the St. Lawrence colony in 1646, to Huronia in 1648, and was martyred in March, 1649. (Thwaites, *op. cit.*)

There have been violent scholarly arguments about Huronia's origin. Frank Ridley suggests that pre-historic Iroquoian people lived in or near Huronia for a long time before French contact, in "Huron and Lalonde Occupations of Ontario," *AA* XVII (1952); "The Fallis Site, Ontario," *AA* XVIII (1952); and "The Forest Bay Site, Lake Nipissing, Ontario," *AA* XX (1954). He sums up his theory in "The Ontario Iroquoian Controversy," *OH* LV (1963). Among those who championed the theory that most Hurons arrived a short time before the French is Bruce Graham Trigger, who has written "The Historic Location of the Hurons," *OH* LIV (1962) and "A Reply to Mr. Ridley," *OH* LV (1963). In his introduction to the 1967 Midland edition of Dr. Tooker's book, however, Mr. Trigger seems to have accepted Mr. Ridley's theory, at least partially.

## Highway to the West

E. Cruikshank, in "An Episode of the War of 1812," *PR* IX (1910) includes material covering development of Yonge Street before the war.

George A. Cuthbertson, *Freshwater*, (Toronto, 1931) tells of the *Griffin* and the early British vessels on the Lakes. DeVoto, *op. cit.*, gives the best over-all treatment of this period. Daniel Williams Harmon, *A Journal of Voyages and Travels* (Andover, 1820) describes canoes, *voyageurs*, and the fur trade. *Alexander Henry's Travels and Adventures* (Chicago, 1921; M. M. Quaife, ed.) gives an early English description of Georgian Bay. Innis, *op. cit.*, has a long chapter on the trade of the Great Lakes and Hudson Bay. Mrs. Anna Jameson, *Winter Studies and Summer Rambles* (London, 1838), describes Fort LaCloche as it was in the 1830's; it must have been much the same in earlier years, and so I have followed her description. Alexander Mackenzie, *Voyages from Montreal* (London, 1801) lists the portages of the French River and describes the fur trade. Eric W. Morse, *Canoe Routes of the Voyageurs* (St. Paul & Toronto, 1962) tells much about both the routes and men, as does Grace Lee Nute, *The Voyageur* (St. Paul, 1955). *The Explorations of Pierre Esprit Radisson* (Minneapolis, 1961; Arthur T. Adams, ed.) is the account by the young man of his travels. Percy J. Robinson, "More About Toronto," *OH* XLV (1953), traces the history of the name. *The Correspondence of Lieut. Governor John Graves Simcoe* (Toronto, 1923; E. A. Cruikshank, ed.) in five volumes gives the picture of Upper Canada in Simcoe's day. Ernest Voorhis, *Historic Forts and Trading Posts* (Department of the Interior, Ottawa, 1930) is an encyclopaedic listing and description of forts, posts, and routes used by the French and British trading companies.

The account by Radisson of his travels with Groseilliers has been interpreted, amended, and reworked by so many authorities that if we accept all the changes it becomes meaningless. I assume that, as Radisson says, he actually went on the first voyage with Groseilliers, a point that has been disputed.

Several wrecks about the Lakes have been called the *Griffin*. One possibility was found in a cove on Russell Island, MacGregor Channel, near Tobermory. C. H. J. Snider, the marine historian, in "Further Search for the Griffon," *OH* XLVIII (1956), concludes, "Until something incontestably belonging to the *Griffon* is found elsewhere it will be very difficult to prove that the Tobermory remains are not hers." (Mr. Snider prefers the alternate spelling.)

Anyone who tried to bypass the French River portages found the rapids deadly. Doris K. Megill, in "Underwater Finds in the French River," *CGJ* LXVII (1963), tells of various objects brought up by divers who searched the river bottom just below some of the rapids. These objects ranged from French trade goods and muskets to cameras and an outboard motor.

Simcoe's official title was Lieutenant-Governor; his duties, however, were those of governor of the province of Upper Canada. He reported directly to the Governor-General of Canada, Lord Dorchester. He often is called Governor Simcoe because that title more correctly suggests his responsibilities. I have used that form. On March 17th, 1794, Simcoe wrote to Dorchester, urging the need for a post on Georgian Bay. Two years later, on May 20th, 1796, he specifically asked for troops to be stationed at Penetanguishene. Dorchester, on the 9th of June, replied, "No more Military Posts appear to me necessary for the present, than have already been declared on Orders. . . ." In August 1796, Simcoe, who had disagreed more and more with Dorchester, sailed for England and never returned. We may speculate on the course of the War of 1812 on the Upper Lakes had Simcoe's desires been met, and a base established then at Penetang.

## 1812

Howard I. Chapelle, in *American Small Sailing Craft* (New York, 1951), discusses the *bateau* as a type of boat, and in his *History of the American Sailing Navy* (New York, 1949) considers the vulnerability of the small Great Lakes naval vessels to boat attack. E. Cruikshank, in "'An Episode of the War of 1812," cited previously, gives material covering McDouall's *bateau* expedition to Mackinac, and the events of 1814 on Georgian Bay; he reprints most of the pertinent British and American documents. William Dunlop, M.D., *Recollections of the American War, 1812-14* (Toronto, 1905) records Dunlop's adventures in clearing the Penetang Road. Alec R. Gilpin's *The War of 1812 in the Old Northwest* (East Lansing, Michigan, 1958) contains an American appraisal of the war on Georgian Bay and at Mackinac. George Head, *Forest Scenes and Incidents in the Wilds of North America* (London, 1829) tells of Head's experiences. J. Mackay Hitsman, *The Incredible War of 1812* (Toronto, 1965) is an excellent military history. Innis, *op. cit.*, also tells of the use of Yonge Street by the fur traders. A. C. Osborne, "Old Penetanguishene," *PP* nos. 5 & 6 (1912 & 1917) gives additional information about the Toronto Passage and Penetang Road. Percy J. Robinson, "Yonge Street and the North West Company," *CHR* XXIV (1943) reviews development of that route and debunks the story that the Northwesters took boats on wheels over Yonge Street. William Wood (ed.), *Select British Documents of the Canadian War of 1812* (Toronto, 1920), III, contains Georgian Bay material.

Sir James Yeo in a letter to Sir George Prevost, 26 November 1814, said that he planned to build a 44-gun frigate at Penetanguishene. He enclosed a report by Lieutenant Poyntz, R.N., which said, "The harbour is one of the finest I ever saw." (PAC, CO 42, vol 157.)

A reminder may be in order that Mackinac is pronounced Mackinaw. See Ernest H. Rankin, "Michilimackinac," *IS* XIV (1958) and Walter Havighurst, *Three Flags at the Straits*, (Englewood Cliffs, N.J., 1966).

## Penetanguishene

James P. Barry, "The Meaning of the Word Lines," *OH* LVIII (1966) tells of the Church of St. James and its location. Chapelle's *History of the American Sailing Navy* gives a plan of the sister vessels *Tecumseth* and *Newash*, moved to Penetang after the war. D. C. Crieghton, *The Commercial Empire of the Saint Lawrence, 1750-1860* (New Haven, 1937) discusses the impact of the war and the peace on the fur trade. Franklin tells briefly of his stop at Penetang in the introduction to his *Narrative of a Second Expedition to the Shores of the Polar Sea* (Philadelphia, 1828). A. F. Hunter, *A History of Simcoe County* (Barrie, Ont., 1909), tells of the Nottawasaga forts and of Penetanguishene. Mrs. Anna Jameson's account is in *Winter Studies and Summer Rambles in Canada*, cited previously. J. K. Johnson, "Chelsea Pensioners in Upper Canada," *OH* LIII (1961) tells of commuted pensioners, but not specifically those at Penetang. The best concise reference of Pentanguishene, and one which at this writing contains the latest results of both archaeological and historical study, is Elsie McLeod Jury's and Wilfrid Jury's *The Establishments at Penetanguishene* (London, Ontario, 1959). Paul Kane, in *Wanderings of an Artist Among the Indians of North America* (London, 1859), speaks of the naval vessels on Georgian Bay in 1845. G. F. Lamb, *Franklin—Happy Voyager* (London, 1956), quotes the letter being written by Franklin to his wife when he learned of her death. Osborne's "Old Penetanguishene," cited previously, contains a great store of basic information about the town gleaned by its author over many years of discussions with old inhabitants and researches on the ground. A. C. Osborne also compiled and annotated "The Migration of Voyageurs from Drummond Island to Penetanguishene," *PR* III (1901). John Philp,

171

"The Economic and Social Effects of the British Garrisons on the Development of Western Upper Canada," *OH* XLI (1949) provides background. Reuben Gold Thwaites (ed.), "The Bulger Papers," *Collections* of the State Historical Society of Wisconsin, XIII (1895), contains a letter from McDouall to Bulger, telling his feelings about the treaty. W. R. Williams, "The Mohawk," *IS* VII (1951), tells of that gunboat.

Despite McDouall's annoyance with the treaty his views were well balanced. He commented, "The irritation & sullen dislike, still subsisting & likely to subsist between the two Countries require the utmost prudence and caution, lest we inadvertently sow the seeds of a new war, & heavy would be the responsibility thereof."

## Red Land and White

Louis Agassiz, *Lake Superior: Its Physical Character, Vegetation, and Animals, With A Narrative of the Tour By J. Elliot Cabot* (Boston, 1850) tells of the meeting with Major Rains. Miss Soaphy Anderson, "The Journey of the First White Settlement Across the Georgian Bay," *MD* I (1921) tells of the trip from Coldwater to Manitoulin. F. H. Armstrong, "Toronto's First Railway Venture, 1834-1838," *OH* LVIII (1966) contains the early plans for a line to the Nottawasaga. "The Manitoulin Letters of the Rev. Charles Crosbie Brough," *OH* XLVIII (1946) tells of the trip also described by Miss Anderson. William Cullen Bryant, *Letters of a Traveller* (New York, 1850) contains the comment on Rains. The basic summary of land policies contributing to the revolt in Upper Canada is found in *The Report and Despatches of the Earl of Durham* (London, 1839). Fred C. Hamil, "An Early Settlement on St. Joseph Island," *OH*, LIII (1961) tells of Major Rains' activities. Hunter, *op. cit.*, gives information on Indian treaties, early settlement, and land-grant policies. Mrs. Jameson, *op. cit.*, describes the meetings with the Indians and the conditions on the island at that time. William H. G. Kingston, *Western Wanderings or, A Pleasure Tour in the Canadas* (London, 1856), gives a clear picture of the way Georgian Bay looked to an outsider in 1853. His superior manner grates at times, but his descriptions seem quite accurate. Fred Landon, *Lake Huron* (New York, 1944) discusses Head's part in consolidating the tribes on Manitoulin. E. L. Marsh, *A History of the County of Grey* (Owen Sound, 1931), tells of the first settlements in the Thornbury-Sydenham area. Osborne tells in "Old Penetanguishene" of the Penetang Road and in "Migration of the Voyageurs" of the first settlement by *voyageurs* in the vicinity. Mrs. S. Rowe, "Anderson Record," *PR* VI (1905) gives a biography of Captain Anderson. Russell D. Smith, "The Northern Railway: Its Origin and Construction, 1834-1885," *OH* XLVIII (1956) gives the history of the first railway to reach Georgian Bay. George Sneath, "A Few Notes on the Township of Sunnidale," *PP* No. 1 (1908), tells of the first settlers along the Nottawasaga. C. H. J. Snider, "Riddle of the Sands' Gave Collingwood Railway," *The Telegram* (Toronto), September 25, 1937, describes the wreck of the *Bishop*. The Rev. Thomas Williams, "Memories of a Pioneer," *PP* No. 2 (1908) tells much about early settlement of Simcoe County (including the passage quoted), and of events along the Nottawasaga during the 1820's.

When the rail line to Georgian Bay was first built, its official name was the Ontario, Simcoe, and Huron Union Railway. Its popular name from the beginning, however, was the Northern Railway. After financial difficulties it was reorganized in 1859 and officially became the Northern Railway. (Hunter, *op. cit.*) For simplicity, I have called it the Northern throughout.

C. H. J. Snider, in his article on the *Bishop*, discusses the rumours, current at the time, that land speculators of Collingwood arranged the wreck at the Nottawasaga to discredit the harbour there.

## Treaty of 1836, (See pp. 49-52.)

MY CHILDREN:

Seventy snow seasons have now passed away since we met in Council at the crooked place (Niagara), at which time and place your Great Father, the King, and the Indians of North America tied their hands together by the wampum of friendship.

Since that period various circumstances have occurred to separate from your Great Father many of his red children, and as an unavoidable increase of white population, as well as the progress of cultivation, have had the natural effect of impoverishing your hunting grounds it has become necessary that new arrangements should be entered into for the purpose of protecting you from the encroachments of the whites.

In all parts of the world farmers seek for uncultivated lands as eagerly as you, my red children, hunt in your forest for game. If you would cultivate your land it would then be considered your own property, in the same way as your dogs are considered among yourselves to belong to those who have reared them; but uncultivated land is like wild animals, and your Great Father, who has hitherto protected you, has now great difficulty in securing it for you from the whites, who are hunting to cultivate it.

Under these circumstances, I have been obliged to consider what is best to be done for the red children of the forest, and I now tell you my thoughts.

It appears that these islands on which we are now assembled in Council are, as well as all those on the north shore of Lake Huron, alike claimed by the English, the Ottawas and the Chippewas.

I consider that from their facilities and from their being surrounded by innumerable fishing islands, they might be made a most desirable place of residence for many Indians who wish to be civilized, as well as to be totally separated from the whites; and I now tell you that your Great Father will withdraw his claim to these islands and allow them to be applied for that purpose.

Are you, therefore, the Ottawas and Chippewas, willing to relinquish your respective claims to these islands and make them the property (under your Great Father's control) of all Indians whom he shall allow to reside on them; if so, affix your marks to this my proposal.

MANITOWANING, 9th August, 1836.    F. B. HEAD,
J. B. ASSEKINACK,
MOKOMMUNISH, (totem),
TAWACKKUCK,
KIMEWEN (totem),
KITCHEMOKOMON (totem),
PESCIATAWICK (totem),
PAIMAUSEGAI (totem),
NAINAWMUTTEBE (totem),
MOSUNEKO (totem),
KEWUCKANCE (totem),
SHAWENAUSEWAY (totem),
ESPANOILE (totem),
SNAKE (totem),
PAUTUNSEWAY (totem),
PAIMAUQUMESTCAM (totem),
WAGEMAUQUIN (totem).

*To the Saukings:*

MY CHILDREN,

You have heard the proposal I have just made to the Chippewas and Ottawas, by which it has been agreed between them and your Great Father that these islands (Manatoulin), on which we are now assembled, should be made, in Council, the property (under your Great Father's control) of all Indians whom he shall allow to reside on them.

I now propose to you that you should surrender to your Great Father the Sauking Territory you at present occupy, and that you should repair either to this island or to that part of your territory which lies on the north of Owen Sound, upon which proper houses shall be built for you, and proper assistance given to enable you to become civilized and to cultivate land, which your Great Father engages for ever to protect for you from the encroachments of the whites.

Are you, therefore, the Sauking Indians, willing to accede to this arrangement; if so, affix your marks to this my proposal.

MANITOWANING, 9th August, 1836.

Witness:

T. G. ANDERSON, *S.I.A.*,  
JOSEPH STINSON, *Genl. Supt. of Wes-  
leyan Missions*,  
ADAM ELLIOT,  
JAMES EVANS,  
F. L. INGALL, *Lieut. 15th Regt.  
Commandg. Detacht.*,  
TALFOURD W. FIELD, *Dist. Agent.*

F. B. HEAD,  
METIEWABE (totem),  
ALEXANDER (totem) KAQUTA BUNE-  
VAIREAR,  
KOWGISAWIS (totem),  
METTAWANSH (totem).

(*Reprinted through the courtesy of the Indian Affairs Branch of the Department of Indian Affairs and Northern Development*)

## The Bay Develops

E. E. Armstrong, "Sketches from the Early History of Parry Sound," Parry Sound Historical Society, 1920 (a paper available from the Parry Sound Public Library), provides general coverage of that district. Canada, *Sessional Papers*, 1863, V; and 1864, IV, contain material on the Manitoulin Island treaty. Samuel Phillips Day, *English America* (London, 1864), gives Georgian Bay material and an eye-witness description of the treaty signing. John Disturnell, *A Trip Through the Lakes of North America* (New York, 1857), gives the description of Collingwood quoted. William Sherwood Fox, *The Bruce Beckons* (Toronto, 1952), tells much of the problems faced by early settlers on the Bruce and of the slaughter of pigeons. His "When Sir John A. Put His Foot Down," *IS* XI (1955) tells of logging on the Bruce and of the difficulties it caused settlers. Miss F. Gladstane, "Fifty Years Reminiscenses and Recollections of Midland," *MD* II (1922) tells of the early settlement of Midland. Kingston, *op. cit.*, describes Collingwood before the railway came, the Bay shore in 1853, and tells the first part of the story of George and Little Current. A. R. M. Lower, *The North American Assault on the Canadian Forest* (Toronto, 1938), contains much information on the development of Georgian Bay. Marsh, *op. cit.*, quotes the story of the mice by an anonymous settler and provides much detail on pioneer life. Fleetwood K. McKean, "Early Parry Sound and the Beatty Family," *OH* LVI (1964) gives a complete picture of the beginnings of Parry Sound and of its founder. He also tells of the railway in "Depot Harbour—the First Seaway Terminal," *IS* XXI (1965). Frederick Wm. Major (compiler), *Manitoulin: the Isle of the Ottawas* (Gore Bay, Ont., 1934) describes events surrounding the Manitoulin Island Treaty. Jesse Edgar Middleton and

Fred Landon, *The Province of Ontario* (Toronto, 1927) II, tells of the be-
ginnings of Bay towns and gives the quotation from the Missionary Report
of the Wesleyan Methodist Church. Margaret H. Mitchell, *The Passenger
Pigeon in Ontario* (Toronto, 1935) discusses the birds at length. Frank
A. Myers, "History of the Hudson's Bay Company Post at Little Current,
Ontario," *IS* XV (1959) & XVI (1960), tells of the post and the later history
of George's undertaking. Mr. Myers' "Historic Sites Marked in Manitoulin
Region," *IS* XVI (1960), contains a résumé of events before and after the
signing of the Indian treaty. George R. Osborne compiled a book, parts of
which he wrote himself, called *A Story of Early Midland and Her Pioneers*
(Midland, 1939). It contains much of the information about Midland I have
used, including the quotation from an old-timer. W. C. Pollard, *Pioneering
in the Prairie West* (Toronto, c. 1926), tells of the Parry Sound colonies that
settled near Edmonton. A. H. Ross, *Reminiscences of North Sydenham*
(Owen Sound, 1924) is a good small book of local history. W. L. Smith
compiled *The Pioneers of Old Ontario* (Toronto, 1923) from stories he heard
as he talked to old inhabitants. It tells of Flora McAlmon. James White,
F.R.G.S., "Place-Names on Georgian Bay," *PR* XI (1913) gives the origin
of the name of Byng Inlet. David Williams, "Shipping on the Upper Lakes,"
*Papers and Records*, Huron Institute (Collingwood, Ont.) I (1909), contains information on early local steamers. W. R. Williams, "The Maganettawan," *IS* X (1954) gives the history of that vessel. *The York Herald*,
July 31 and Aug 7, 1863 (OPA) tells of the policemen landing on Manitoulin and the events that followed.

The unfortunate Hon. John Byng, Admiral of the Blue, for whom Byng
Inlet was named, was shot in 1757 because he failed to relieve Minorca the
preceding year, although the fault was in fact that of his government. Dudley
Pope, in *At Twelve Mr. Byng Was Shot* (New York, 1962) says "The trial
and execution of Admiral the Hon. John Byng was one of the most cold-
blooded and cynical acts of judicial murder in all British history." Lieutenant Bayfield (later an admiral himself), who named the inlet during his
surveys of 1820-3, must have agreed.

The quotation on passenger pigeons by C. A. Fleming is taken from the
appendix of Margaret Mitchell's book, in which she reprints an article by
Mr. Fleming that appeared in the *Owen Sound Daily Sun Times*, April 11,
1931. She also quotes the description by Judge Latchford.

The dates of the last pigeons seen on Georgian Bay are given by Dr. Fox
in *The Bruce Beckons*.

## The Falling of the Pine

D. D. Calvin, *A Saga of the Saint Lawrence* (Toronto, 1945) tells much
of the movement of squared timbers from the Lakes to Quebec. Chapelle's
*American Small Sailing Craft* describes lumbermen's *bateaux* and gives
plans of them. James Elliott Defebaugh, in *History of the Lumber Industry
of America* (Chicago, 1906), discusses Georgian Bay lumbering and reviews government manœuvres affecting the export of logs. *Memoirs of
Robert Dollar* (San Francisco, 1918) gives Dollar's experiences and contains
the passages quoted. Fox, *The Bruce Beckons* and "When Sir John A. Put
His Foot Down," tell of logging on the Bruce. A little booklet published
by the Georgian Bay Development Association, *Designated Area Legislation
in the Georgian Bay Region* (Midland, 1966) tells of government conces-
sions to businesses that locate in "Designated Areas"—those economically
depressed—and announces that "In all of Ontario there are only 10 Areas
Designated under this New Legislation. . . . Six of these Areas are in the
Georgian Bay Region," thus pointing up the economic situation since the

end of the lumber boom. Edwin C. Guillet, *Early Life in Upper Canada* (Toronto, 1963), has a full chapter on Canadian logging. Stewart H. Holbrook's *Holy Old Mackinaw* (New York, 1938), is the most readable, amusing, and informative book about the American logger; what he says is also true about Georgian Bay loggers in the 80's and later, when the two nationalities mingled on both sides of the Lakes. Hunter, *op. cit.*, gives information on mills and logging along the Georgian Bay shore of Simcoe County. Robert C. Johnson, in "Rafts for Saginaw," *IS* V (1949) provides a detailed history of the rafting business and its methods. Lower, *op. cit.*, has much on Georgian Bay lumbering. Captain James McCannel, in "Shipping Out of Collingwood," *PR* XXVIII (1932) lists the cargoes of the first steamers from Collingwood to Chicago. Lumber and various wood products are included. McKean, "Early Parry Sound and the Beatty Family," tells of Parry Sound lumbering. Cameron McLeod, "The Ghost of Sandy Gray," *MD* II (1922). Charles Macnamara's "The Camboose Shanty," *OH* LI (1959) gives a full description. *MD* II (1922) provides a short history of James Playfair's business activities at Midland. Franz Rickaby, *Ballads and Songs of the Shanty-Boy* (Cambridge, Mass., 1926) contains the song quoted. Marlow A. Shaw's delightful book, *The Happy Islands* (Toronto, 1926), has a chapter on Georgian Bay logging and tells of Sandy Gray. W. R. Williams, "Big Tugs and Big Rafts," *IS* III (1947), describes lumbering on Georgian Bay. It is this article that gives 1940 as the end of the industry on the Bay. The same author, in "The Georgian Bay Survey of 1885-1888," *IS* XIII (1957) mentions lumber schooners sailing from Port Severn as early as 1850. Mr. Williams, in "John Island's Stolen Sawmill," *IS* VIII (1952), tells at length of the stolen mill.

Franz Rickaby heard the song, *The Falling of the Pine*, sung by an old-timer in Minnesota. Rickaby traces it to Georgian Bay and the early period of square-timber logging. It is quite sophisticated for a logger's song, with internal rhymes and big words. One stanza refers to the sun as "bright Phœbus." Needless to say, when the boys got to that it often came out strangely; in one version it even became "Feeble Phœbie."

The information about the local name of the Big Red Mill at Collingwood and about the lowering of the water level in the Nottawasaga River is contained in a letter to me from Captain William Watts, of the Collingwood boatbuilding family, written from San Diego, California, on December 19, 1938. Captain Watts was then in his seventies.

Chapelle, in *American Small Sailing Craft*, calls the lumbermen's craft *bateaux*. Lower uses the name pointer interchangeably with *bateau*, as the Ontario lumbermen did.

The history of Sandy Gray is one of those hard-to-pin-down semi-folk stories. Shaw gives three slightly differing versions; Cameron McLeod tells a fourth. The skeptical reader may note a resemblance to the classic loggers' ballad, *The Jam on Garry's Rock*, in which "four of our Canadian boys" (with their foreman, young Monroe) volunteered to break the jam on a Sunday, even though others did not think they should work that day; of course the Canadian boys and their foreman were carried away when the jam broke. The date given for Sandy's death is also conveniently early, so that the legend becomes obscured in the haze of time past. On the other hand, there evidently was a Sandy Gray; many people seem to have known him and there was a grave along the Musquosh marked with his name.

## Canoes, Sails, and Fishing Craft

Edwin Tappan Adney and Howard I. Chapelle, *The Bark Canoes and Skin Boats of North America* (Smithsonian Institution, Washington, 1964) is the definitive reference. Louis Frechette, *Christmas in French Canada* (Toronto, 1899) contains the passage quoted. Judge F. W. Howay, "Building the Big Canoes," *The Beaver*, December 1939, tells of Hudson's Bay Company canoes. Lower, *op. cit.*, describes the adaptation of canoes and *bateaux* from the fur trade to the lumber trade. Grace Lee Nute, *op. cit.*, has a chapter on canoes. Sagard, *op cit.*, gives the description of Huron canoes.

Hunter, *op cit.*, tells of the *Gore*. Jury & Jury, *The Establishments at Penetanguishene*, tell of the gunboats built on the Nottawasaga. Paul Kane, *op. cit.*, refers to the vessel that sailed from Sturgeon Bay to Sydenham as a "packet," thus inferring regular sailings. J. M. Kilbourn, "Reminiscences of the First Settlers of Owen Sound," *PR* XVIII (1920) gives a more complete description of that sloop. McCannel, *op. cit.*, tells of sailing vessels, including the *Malta*. *MD* II (1922) contains photographs of Midland, Collingwood, and Owen Sound harbours *sans* sailing vessels. Myers, "History of the Hudson's Bay Post at Little Current, Ontario," tells of the wild drunk at Little Current. Osborne, "Old Penetanguishene," tells of Stephen Jeffrey's schooner, and "Migration of the Voyageurs" describes the *Alice Hackett* wreck. James H. Rutherford, "Early Navigation on the Georgian Bay," *PR* XVIII (1920), describes the early vessels launched at Sydenham. Shaw, *op. cit.*, tells of the signboard on Jane McLeod Island. C. H. J. Snider, " 'Annavann' in the Great Gale of 1880," *The Telegram* (Toronto) July 27, 1946; and "The *Otonabee*'s Tough Time," *The Telegram*, December 24, 1937, tells the story of the schooner and the captain's wife. Mr. Snider's "Ripples Over the *Nellie Sherwood*," *The Telegram*, July 23, 1938, discusses that schooner and quotes Robert Lymburner. W. R. Williams, "Historic Hope Island," *The Free Press Herald* (Midland), December 19, 1945, gives the date of the wreck of the *Lottie Wolf*. His "Lumber Carriers of the Lakes," *IS* XI (1955) describes the method of loading lumber.

John Disturnell, *A Trip Through the Lakes of North America*, mentions the lighthouse at Collingwood in 1857. W. Gibbard, "The First Trip of the *Rescue*," *The Daily Globe*, (Toronto) July 21, 1858 (PAC), in a letter to the editor tells of the Cove Island Light in that year. H. L. Harley, "A Cruise to Georgian Bay," *The Rudder* X (1899), describes the lighthouse keeper he visited. J. B. Mansfield (ed.), *History of the Great Lakes* (Chicago, 1899) I, tells of the damage and reconstruction at Collingwood. W. R. Williams, "Georgian Bay's First Lighthouse Centennial," *IS* XII (1956) tells of Christian Island Light and gives the dates other lights were established.

Paul James Barry, "Mackinaw Boats and Collingwood Skiffs," *Yachting*, LXVIII (1940) describes the boats and gives their history in detail, based on interviews with some of the old-timers and on a lengthy correspondence with the son of the boatbuilder, Captain William Watts, who then was living on the Pacific Coast. (The article was written by me under a youthful combination of names.) Howard I. Chapelle, *American Small Sailing Craft*, also discusses these boats. Daniel Cuchin & Henry A. Regier, *Dynamics and Exploitation of Lake Whitefish in Southern Georgian Bay* (ODLF, 1965) is an extensive study that concludes the area may be on the verge of over-fishing. Disturnell, *A Trip Through the Lakes of North America*, gives the material quoted. Fox, *The Bruce Beckons*, tells of Lake Huron fishermen on northern Georgian Bay. James Cleland Hamilton, *The Georgian Bay* (Toronto, 1893), gives much on commercial fisheries of the time, including the passage quoted. Kingston, *op. cit.*, speaks of fishing at Manitoulin. George H. McIvor, *Report of Commission of Inquiry into Freshwater Fish Marketing* (Ottawa, 1965?), contains an excellent section on the history of fishing on the Great Lakes, including Georgian Bay. H. H. MacKay, *Fishes of Ontario* (ODLF, 1963), presents technical material in readable form. Marsh, *op. cit.*, tells the story of fishing boats mistaken for an invading fleet. ODLF, "Record of Commercial Fish Production in Georgian Bay 1871-1960," and "Statistics of the Commercial Fishery in Georgian Bay, 1946 to 1965," are both useful statistical tables. A. C. Osborne, "The Migration of Voyageurs," mentions early fishing near Penetang. George R. Osborne, *op. cit.*, tells of fishing at Midland. W. H. R. Werner & M. J. Brubacher, *Fisheries Management in Georgian Bay* (Technical Bulletin, Fish and Wildlife Series #10, ODLF, 1960) discuss the lamprey problem and possible solutions.

According to Cuthbertson, *op. cit.*, the *Annie and Jane*, having once passed through the Welland Canal, returned to Lake Ontario. She could hardly have made another trip and proceeded to Georgian Bay that season. A. C. Osborne, who mentions the story that the Jeffery schooner was the first through the canal, also discounts it.

The series of articles by C. H. J. Snider that appeared for many years in *The Telegram* under the general title "Schooner Days" contains an unequalled collection of stories about ships and shipping, many of them dealing with Georgian Bay.

The Christian Island Lighthouse, after some vicissitudes, now has an unwatched beacon mounted at the top of its tower. The old many-windowed lantern has been removed. The stone walls of the dwelling remain as a roofless shell.

The letter of Captain Watts containing the passage quoted was written to me from San Diego, California, on April 2, 1939.

## The First Steamers

The best overall histories of Georgian Bay shipping are those by Capt. James McCannel, James H. Rutherford, and David Williams, all cited previously. The most authoritative and concise story of the vessels used before 1900 is Captain McCannel's.

The following references deal with the subjects shown. Canada, *Sessional Papers*, XIII, 1880 (*Waubuno*). J. H. Coyne, "Across Georgian Bay in 1871," *PR* XXVIII (1932) (passengers making round trip to Lake Superior). Day, *op. cit.* (describes briefly the commerce of Collingwood in 1862). John Disturnell, *The Great Lakes* (New York, 1863) (*Rescue*); *Sailing on the Great Lakes and Rivers of America* (Philadelphia, 1874) (Collingwood route and advertisement of Lake Superior Royal Mail Line); *A Trip Through the Lakes of North America* (Early Collingwood-Chicago steamers). *Evergreen City Times* (Sheboygan, Wisc.) Sept. 27, Oct. 4 & 25, 1856 (Mead Public Library, Sheboygan) (*Niagara* disaster). Gibbard, *op. cit.* (*Rescue*). Hunter, *op. cit.* (*Gore*). *IS* XI (1955) (contains photos of the *Chicora, Frances Smith*, and *Waubuno*). Mrs. Jameson, *op. cit.*, (*Penetanguishene*). Kingston, *op. cit.* (*Kaloolah*). William A. McDonald (ed.), "Eye Witness Reports of the Burning of the *Niagara*," *IS* XII (1956). Fleetwood K. McKean, "Early Parry Sound and the Beatty Family," (*Waubuno*); "The Wreck of the *S.S. Waubuno*," *IS* XXI (1965). Guy MacLean, "The *Georgian* Affair; an Incident of the American Civil War," *CHR* XLII (1961). Marsh, *op. cit.* (*Ploughboy*). Mansfield, *op. cit.*, I (*Waubuno*). *MD* I (1922), "Members of Parliament Pray for Deliverance," (*Ploughboy*). Laurence Oliphant, *Minnesota and the Far West* (London, 1845) (Boarding ship at Sturgeon Bay). A. C. Osborne, "The Migration of Voyageurs" (*Penetanguishene*). William Ratigan, *Great Lakes Shipwrecks & Survivals* (Grand Rapids, Mich., 1960) (*Waubuno*). Robert W.

Thom, "The Wreck of the *Mary Ward*," *IS* IV (1948) (contains the anon. account I have quoted). TBHS, *Fourteenth Annual Report* (1923), "The Steamer *Rescue*." James White, *op. cit.*, (*Gore*). W. R. Williams, "The *Maganettawan*," and "The *Ploughboy*," *IS* X (1954). Anna G. Young, "The Rough Diamond," *IS* XVIII (1962) (Capt. Peter Campbell).

James P. Barry, "The Wolseley Expedition Crosses the Great Lakes," *IS* XXIV (1968) gives a detailed account, with complete references.

General background for this period is provided by Middleton and Landon, *op. cit.*, and Carl Wittke, *A History of Canada* (New York, 1928).

The log house mentioned by Antoine Labatte still stands at this writing. For many years it has been used as a summer cottage.

It is Captain McCannel's estimate that 150 persons were lost on the *Niagara*.

## The Fleets Come—and Go

McCannel, Rutherford, and David Williams again provide the general references. That of Mr. Williams is particularly useful in tracing development of the shipping companies.

References on specific subjects are as follows. Richard Bissell, "Oh Keewatin!" *Holiday*, August 1966, is a humorous, impressionistic account of a voyage on the C.P.R. steamer. It is Bissell who compares the dockside at Port McNicoll to the set of a British musical comedy. Dana Thomas Bowen, *Memories of the Lakes* (Daytona Beach, 1946) (*Asia* photo). John A. Burke and Cletus P. Schneider, letter, *IS* XXII (1966) (last C.P.R. passenger voyage). Canada, *Sessional Papers*, XVI, 1883 (*Asia* and *Manitoulin*). Cuthbertson, *op. cit.* (C.P.R. vessels). *DMH* II (1949), "The Glen Line" (Playfair fleets); "The Dominion-Owen Sound Fleet." *DMH* X (1957) "Ships of the Northern Navigation Company." Herbert W. Dosey, "Algoma Argosy," *IS* X (1954) (*Norgoma*). The Rev. Edward J. Dowling, S. J. "Canada-Atlantic Transit Co.," *DMH* XVIII (1965); "Canadian Pacific Railway," *DMH* XV (1962). Fred Landon, "The End of Coastal Steamer Service on Georgian Bay," *IS* XI (1955) (*Midland City*, etc.); *Lake Huron* (quotation from Manitoulin Island paper on steamer race; dates of deaths of *Asia* survivors); "The *Midland City*," *IS* VIII (1952). Bernard McEvoy, *From the Great Lakes to the Wide West*, (Toronto, 1902) (voyage on *Athabasca*). Fleetwood K. McKean, "Depot Harbour—The First Seaway Terminal;" "Early Parry Sound and the Beatty Family;" "Oscar Wing—a Captain of the Lakes," *IS* XXII (1966). James McLaughlin, Sr., "Reminiscences of Owen Sound and its District," *PR* XVIII (1920) (dredges for Owen Sound). Gordon Macaulay, "Ferries out of Owen Sound," *IS* XXI (Dominion & Owen Sound Lines). Mansfield, *op. cit.*, I (*Manitoulin, Asia*). Lorenzo Marcolin, "Canadian Pacific Railway Company Steamship Lines—Last of an Era," *IS* XXII (1966). *MD* I (1921) "The Wreck of the 'Asia'." *MD* II (1922) "Midland's Semi-Centennial" (Playfair enterprises). George R. Osborne, *op. cit.* (Playfair enterprises). Ratigan, *op. cit.* (*Manitoulin*). Albert F. Sprock, "The *Norisle* of Owen Sound and Tobermory," *IS* XXII (1966). Robert W. Thom, "The Sinking of the *Ottawa*," *IS* IX (1953). Dunk Tinkiss, "Dunk Tinkiss Tells His Story," *MD* I (1921) (*Asia*, including passage quoted). W. R. Williams, "*City of Dover*," *DMH* XIV (1961); "The Foundering of *Manasoo* and *Hibou*," *IS* XV (1959); "James Playfair," *DMH* XIII (1960); "The New England Transportation Company," *IS* XIV (1958); "The Northwest Transportation Company," *IS* XVIII (1962). Anna G. Young, *Great Lakes' Saga* (Owen Sound, 1965) (H. H. Gildersleeve & many steamer photos); "The Rough Diamond" (Capt. Campbell; *Manitoulin*).

The summary of the official report of investigation of the loss of the *Asia*, by Capt. P. A. Scott, R.N., concluded, "The vessel appears to have been too light forward, and therefore unable to luff when the gale struck her, but had to bear its whole force on her broadside. It also appears that she had not sufficient cargo in her hold to enable a vessel of her description, with lofty upper works, to stand up against the gale." (*Sessional Papers*, cited above.)

A photograph of the carriage owned by Mr. and Mrs. James Playfair, standing in front of their house, is in the collection of the Huronia Museum, Midland. Until recently that museum occupied the old Playfair house.

Some recollections of the Playfairs are those of my parents and grandparents; some recollections of the *Midland City* are my own.

## The Pleasure-Seekers

Barlow Cumberland, *The Northern Lakes of Canada* (Toronto, 1886) discusses vacationing on Georgian Bay. *Forest and Stream* LII (April 8 & 15, 1899) "A Sailing Dinghy," tells of the dinghy designed for the Bay. Filomena Gould, "A Sixth Great Lake," *IS* XXIII (1967), gives the recreational history of Pointe au Baril. *Guide to Muskoka Lakes, Upper Maganetawan & Inside Channel of the Georgian Bay* (Gravenhurst, c. 1895) contains much information for its small size. Harley, *op. cit.*, tells of the yachtsmen's visits to Manitoulin in 1898. Elmes Henderson, "Some Notes on a Visit to Penetanguishene and the Georgian Bay in 1856." *PR* XXVIII (1932), tells of that trip. Capt. Mac, *The Muskoka Lakes and the Georgian Bay* (Ottawa, 1884) speaks of sport fishing, Wasaga Beach and the environs of Collingwood, the islands, and Parry Sound. *Madawaska Club, Go-Home Bay, 1898-1923* (Toronto, 1923) gives the early history of the club. *Muskoka, Land of Health and Pleasure* (Toronto? c. 1896) tells of the canoe trip from Parry Sound to Lake Joseph. *The Northern Lakes Guide* (Toronto, 1879) contains several pages on Georgian Bay. A. C. Osborne, "The Migration of Voyageurs" gives the anecdotes about Mrs. Jameson and Lord Morpeth. George R. Osborne, *op. cit.*, tells of houseboats.

The books by Cumberland and Mac and the last two guidebooks listed, are in the Department of Rare Books and Special Collections, University of Toronto Library.

## Today

Eric R. Axelson, "Collingwood is Unique," *Canadian Shipping* (January, 1956) tells much of the history of the Collingwood Shipyards. Albert G. Ballert, "The Ports and Commerce of Georgian Bay," *IS* XI (1955) is an excellent review as of that date. Ann Davison, *In the Wake of the Gemini* (Boston, 1962), has several chapters on cruising the Trent Waterway, Georgian Bay, and North Channel. Georgian Bay Development Association, *Industrial Handbook* (Midland, 1967) is a directory of all industrial activity; new editions are issued periodically. *IS* XXIII (1967) "Changes in Name and Operation," tells of the christening of the *Feux Follets*. Fred Landon, "Shipbuilding at Midland, Ontario," *IS* VI (1950) describes Midland shipbuilding to that year. Ontario Department of Economics and Development, *Georgian Bay Region* (Toronto, 1963) gives a detailed survey of all economic activity, including tourism. A. C. Osborne, "The Migration of Voyageurs" tells of the casks buried in the sand at Thunder Bay. James M. Ripley, "Hinged Freighters—Concept for the Future?" *IS* XXII (1966) discusses various proposals for building Lake freighters up to 1,000 feet

180

long. Kenneth McNeill Wells's *Cruising the Georgian Bay* (Toronto, 1961) and *Cruising the North Channel* (Toronto, 1960) describe not only the water approaches and harbours, but also what is found ashore; new editions are issued periodically.

Among the moving spirits in establishing the Collingwood Shipyards was Captain Alexander McDougall, the inventive Scot who grew up near Collingwood, moved to the United States, became a Lake Captain, conceived the idea of the whaleback steamer, supervised the building of a number of these vessels, and in time became a rich man through his many business ventures. He was active in setting up the steel shipyard at Collingwood and its subsidiary at Kingston, and retained his interest in these yards until the United States entered the First World War. He then sold out and returned to designing and building ships in the U.S. ("The Autobiography of Captain Alexander McDougall," *IS* XXIV (1968).

Collingwood Shipyards and Ernest Leitz (Canada) Ltd. kindly provided much of the information about their plants and products.

# Index

186

188

189